DICTIONARY OF BRITISH
ANTIQUE GLASS

Also by Douglas Ash

Dictionary of British Antique Glass

DOUGLAS ASH F.S.A.

Pelham Books

First published in Great Britain by
PELHAM BOOKS LTD
52 Bedford Square
London WC1B 3EF
1975

ISBN 0 7207 0837 0

Printed in Great Britain by
Western Printing Services Ltd, Bristol
in Eleven on Twelve Point Bembo
and bound by James Burn at Esher

ACKNOWLEDGEMENTS

The author wishes to thank Miss Judith Day and Mr John P. Cushion, of the Victoria and Albert Museum, London, who kindly read the proofs.

INTRODUCTION

The chief purpose of this book is to make information readily available concerning British glass of the period of most interest to students and amateurs, namely, from the late 16th century to the early 19th century, though previous phases are considered to some extent in order to complete the picture. A large body of literature already exists on the subject, as may be seen from the Bibliography, but the present volume is not intended to replace any of the books in question, but simply to present the facts in a more convenient form. The subject is a vast one, and even the most experienced amateur must remain in some degree a permanent student, as in other branches of applied art, so that this book may well serve his turn in various ways by refreshing his memory. To the comparative newcomer, however, who has had no opportunity of studying the matter in depth and is unfamiliar with technicalities and collectors' jargon, it is hoped that this Dictionary will prove especially useful; for instead of being obliged to pursue some small facet of the subject among many separate pages of an orthodox book, sometimes only to come off scurvily in the end, he will be able, by going straight to the matter that interests him, to satisfy his curiosity with little trouble.

Only one of the previous works on glass has, so far as the present author is aware, been in the form of a dictionary, but its scope was quite different from that of this book, since it carried the story up to recent times. Confining this alphabetical survey to the period mentioned at the beginning of this Introduction has not, of course, been done in despite of modern hand-made glass, much of which is of fine quality, as anyone familiar with the names Whitefriars, Webb & Corbett, Steuben, Orrefors and many others, can readily attest. It has been done in recognition of the circumstance that the interest of most collectors and amateurs, who relish antiquity no less than quality and positive character, ends at about the year 1840.

Individual glasshouses have been discussed only when they are considered as having some special historical significance, and it has been deemed superfluous to provide readers with a detailed recipe for making glass.

Glass-making was an Oriental art introduced into Europe largely by Orientals. It is not possible to determine beyond doubt whether it began in Egypt or Syria or in both countries more or less simultaneously, for it was pursued with vigour in each of these locations from before the middle of the 2nd millennium B.C. One must be wary of chauvinistic special pleading masquerading as careful scholarship on one side or the other, but Egypt has been a general favourite for some years, partly because its culture was greatly superior to anything in Syria in ancient times, partly because sodium carbonate, the alkaline flux employed exclusively for many centuries in the manufacture of fused glass, occurred native in Egypt in large quantities. Sidonian glass-makers were obliged either to import their soda from Egypt, or extract it themselves from the ashes of certain marine plants which also contained lime. What is certain is that one of the most important inventions affecting the craft, the invention of the blowing-tube, occurred in Syria during the 1st century B.C., shortly before the Christian era, and this revolutionized glass-making. When both countries became Roman provinces on the establishment of the Empire under Augustus in 27 B.C., the Egypto-Syrian technical skills began to spread all over the Roman world. In particular, they passed up the valley of the Rhône into Northern Gaul, and encountered such favourable conditions that, by the 2nd century, a glass industry had begun to grow in the area between the Rhine and the Seine which was soon to rival the industries of Alexandria and Sidon. News of this development spread quickly along the political and commercial lifelines, and many Semitic glass-workers, inspired by the financial acumen which has always characterized their branch of the Caucasoid race, considered it worth their while to travel all the way to the Seine-Rhine region to derive profit from participation in the new glass-making boom.

The latter was greatly stimulated by the establishment of viticulture by the Romans in the 3rd century in the now famous wine-producing regions of Rhine-Moselle, Burgundy, Bordeaux and Provence. When the wine began to flow from presses which, by a wry twist of fortune, eventually disgorged better liquor than the legionaries had ever found in their sunnier homelands, all kinds of glass vessels were required to drink it, transport it, and store it.

It is known that in Britain, the most Northerly province of the Roman Empire, glass-making was carried on in a number of places including Colchester (*Camulodunum*); but although it seems probable that other important centres such as York (*Eboracum*), London (*Londinium*) and Lincoln (*Lindum Colonia*) also shared in this activity, this has not yet been proved by archaeological discovery. What seems evident is that glass-making in Roman Britain was not on a very large scale, and that it was found more convenient to import most requirements from the mainland, where the industry was highly organized and competitive.

After the departure of the legions in the middle of the 5th century, traffic with the Continent practically came to an end, for there were no longer any Roman naval escorts to protect merchant ships from the Saxon pirates who swarmed in the narrow seas. When these same predators colonized parts of Western Germany, the Netherlands, and eventually Britain, they did not destroy the Seine-Rhine glass industry but changed its direction. They were not interested in phials, pickle-jars, amphorae, cinerary urns, or many of the other practical or decorative objects which had been in demand under the Roman occupation; but being greatly addicted to the drinking of ale, mead and wine, they required glass cone-beakers and claw-beakers for drinking vessels, as more refined alternatives to huge ox-horns, or as cheaper alternatives to bowls, beakers, or standing cups made of silver.

It used to be widely supposed that no glass-making at all was carried on in Anglo-Saxon England, but this is now known to be incorrect. It undoubtedly occurred in both the North-East and the South-West, and therefore probably in other parts of Britain as well, but unfortunately, little more than this can at present be said. Drinking vessels presumably continued to be made wherever the necessary raw materials were to be had, but there was no competent production of window-glass until over a century and a half after the arrival of another set of Germanic invaders in 1066, this time from Normandy (*See* Laurence Vitrearius).

An archaeological fog shrouds nearly all medieval glass-making in Britain at a time when Venice and Altare were pre-eminent in Europe. Occasional references occurred, and Chaucer, in the late 14th century, describing the Prioress in his *Canterbury Tales*, spoke of 'hire eyen grey as glas'; but whether he was referring to window-glass or vessel-glass, we cannot be sure, though it is commonly assumed that the latter was nearly always green.

Even by 1586, it is clear from William Harrison's *Description of England*, published in that year, that Venetian glass enjoyed greater general prestige than native productions, but events were already afoot which were to bring about a fundamental change in the situation. From this time until the late 17th century, the history of British glass-making is bound up with the names of Jean Carré, Jacopo Verzelini, Sir Jerome Bowes, Sir Robert Mansell, the Duke of Buckingham and George Ravenscroft, all of whom are discussed in the text.

9

A

Absolon, William: an artist, working in Yarmouth in the late 18th and early 19th centuries, who decorated glassware by engraving, enamelling and gilding. Some of his work has been identified by initials, and is pleasing rather than distinguished.

Acid etching: sometimes known incorrectly as 'acid engraving', the decoration of glass by etching it with hydrofluoric acid appears to have been discovered by the engraver Heinrich Schwanhardt of Nürnberg in the late 17th century. In Britain, the technique remained virtually unpractised until the Victorian era, when it was applied to many kinds of useful and decorative wares and to windows and looking-glasses in public houses. On no account should a layman attempt to experiment with hydrofluoric acid. In contact with the flesh it produces most painful and serious lesions, and even the vapour is highly dangerous.

Acorn knop

Acorn knop: a protuberance on the stem of a drinking glass or other appropriate object in a shape suggestive of an acorn, with the wider part at the top. The acorn knop was current in the late 17th and early 18th centuries. The shape was common on Dutch brass candlesticks imported into Britain in large numbers in the early 17th century. *See* Stems.

Adam, Robert: a Scottish architect, born at Kirkcaldy in Fifeshire, who was chiefly responsible for the introduction of the neo-classical style into Britain and Ireland, following his return from a four-year visit to Italy in 1758. This style, which affected all the artistic crafts in varying degree, arose as a result of the discoveries made during the excavations at Herculaneum and Pompeii: two Graeco-Roman cities near Naples which had been overwhelmed simultaneously by an eruption of Mt. Vesuvius in A.D. 79.

Though glassware manifested neo-classical influence to a less degree than architecture, furniture and silver, it was sometimes wheel-engraved with typical motifs such as swags, paterae and urns, while decanters and jugs might occasionally be in the form of classical vases. But perhaps the chief innovation resulting from the new enthusiasm was the rummer (q.v.), the earlier of which were based on classical originals.

Air bubbles: bubbles of air have been found in glass objects from the earliest times to the 19th century and occasionally later, though their incidence declined with the improvement in furnaces in which the ingredients were melted. In the time of Verzelini (q.v.) and in the 17th century they were very numerous and sometimes had the appearance of snowstorms. These minute bubbles are known as 'seeds'. After the introduction of lead crystal, they tended to become fewer and larger, and are sometimes found imprisoned in the substance of large objects like decanters, and in the bowls, stems and feet of drinking glasses. Though recognized as defects, they appear to have been regarded with some tolerance until the 19th century.

Air bubbles introduced deliberately by way of decoration are considered under Tears.

Air-twists: spiralling threads of air in the stems of glasses. In the 18th century, such stems were known as 'wormed shanks'. The technique was invented in England in about 1730 and continued to be applied as a fashionable form of treatment until about 1760. The simplest varieties consisted of multiple fine threads and occurred in glasses made in two pieces, the cylindrical stem being drawn from the base of the bowl. Before the latter was shaped, and while it was still attached to the blowing-tube in the form of a globe, a circuit of deep depressions was

12

made in the thick glass at the opposite end. The plastic glass was then gathered over these depressions, which thus formed bubbles of air which expanded with the heat. The glass was then drawn out and twisted, so that as the stem was elongated the bubbles became lengthened and spiralled. The twists in these two-piece glasses are sometimes described as 'rising into the base of the bowl', but in fact, of course, they descend from the base of the bowl to the bottom of the stem.

In about 1740, knopped air-twists began to appear, usually below a bell-shaped bowl (*See* Bowls), with the top of an inverted baluster (q.v.) beneath a constricted, cylindrical zone from which much of the air had been squeezed out, leaving very fine threads which are often barely discernible and sometimes not visible at all. Such knopped, two-piece glasses are of great rarity, for it was not long before it was found more convenient to make them in three pieces, with the stem fashioned from a length of air-twist rod, having the bowl welded to one end and the foot to the other. The line of the weld between bowl and stem can often be seen, but if not, it is necessary to compare the number of twists, if any, in the base of the bowl with those in the stem in order to determine the type of construction.

Slightly later, double-series twists appeared and consisted, as the name suggests, of one kind of twist spiralling round another in the centre of the stem. Glasses with stems of this type were usually, though not invariably, of three-piece construction, and very seldom displayed knops, whereas two or more knops were fairly common with single-series twist stems, especially in the 1750s.

In about the middle of the century appeared what are described in modern times as mercury twists or mercurial twists. These often consisted of no more than two air spirals, which could naturally be made larger than multiple twists. They do not contain mercury but have great brilliance. Mercury twists were usually accompanied by trumpet-shaped bowls. At about the same time, composite stems began to be made, with air-twist sections combined with other elements. *See* Stems.

Akerman, John: a member of the Glass Sellers' Company of London whose name appeared in an advertisement in the *Whitehall Evening Post* of 27 October 1719, stating that he continued to sell 'Plain and diamond cut flint glasses'. His firm was probably founded in about 1718 in Cornhill, and he moved to Fenchurch Street in 1746, being assisted in the business by his son Isaac. His importance in British glass history lies in the fact that he was responsible for popularizing English cut glass. Of possible German origin or extraction himself, he employed a German cutter named Haedy, and probably several others whose names have not come down to us.

Despite the significance of Akerman's activities it cannot be assumed that he actually introduced cut glass to Great Britain; it was already familiar to the London merchants. But he may have been inspired or stimulated by the attempt by an importer to hold an auction sale of German cut glass in London in 1709. Local glass-sellers attended in force and staged what might be politely termed a demonstration, as a result of which the sale had to be abandoned. Whatever may be thought of the ethics of behaving riotously at an auction, there can be no doubt of the soundness of the move in terms of commercial strategy. If the sale had gone forward, it seems highly probable that a demand would have been created which British glass-makers would have been unable to satisfy, for it appears certain that there were few if any English craftsmen at the time who would have been able to carry out the work. This demand would accordingly have led to increasing foreign intrusions into the British market with detrimental effects on the native industry.

Akerman evidently attained some prominence and was well regarded by his contemporaries, for he was elected Master of the Glass Sellers' Company in 1741, to be followed by his son in 1756. The firm was last heard of in 1785. *See* Cut glass.

Ale or Beer glasses: in this section we are concerned with strong ale or beer which was drunk from glasses, rather than with small beer – a weaker brew which was normally consumed from tankards or mugs of silver, pewter or other materials, and mugs or cans made of glass. The terms 'ale' and 'beer' are now used loosely and are virtually interchangeable, but this was not always the case. In the late 16th century, the distinction drawn between them was based on the fact that beer was flavoured with the 'hoppe' while ale was not. Both, of course, were produced by the action of yeast, a unicellular fungus, on the various sugars composing barley malt. Attempts were made to introduce hops in the 15th century and their use was legalized in 1440, but these attempts were resisted, many maintaining that the plant, which was sometimes called 'this wicked weed', was poisonous. In the early 16th century, however, close contacts with the Flemish portion of the Duchy of Burgundy, an appanage of the Habsburg Empire, stimulated a growing enthusiasm for beer, and hops began to be used as an additive on a greatly increasing scale. The merit of the hop lies in two bitter, aromatic resins, humulon and lupulin, and it was probably soon noticed that their presence gave malt liquor a zestful tang, improved its foaming properties, and acted as a preservative. A song of the late 16th century began with the words 'I gave her cakes and I gave her ale...' and there is no doubt that the liquor continued to be drunk; but in January 1576, Queen Elizabeth I received a present of 'some litell beare glasses', and those concerned with the manufacture or sale of glass in the 17th century mostly used the same phrase rather than the word 'ale'.

Between 1667 and 1673, John Greene of London, an active member of the Glass Sellers' Company (q.v.), sent designs for glasses for the English market to one of the Company's Venetian suppliers, and these included not only stemmed beer vessels like slightly enlarged versions of contemporary glasses for common beverage wine, but also squat beakers somewhat like modern tumblers, but whose height was the same as their width at the top. These might be plain, ribbed, or dotted with vitreous enamel.

A few years later, George Ravenscroft (q.v.), pioneer of English lead-crystal, issued lists which mentioned beer glasses but made no reference to ale, though there is no doubt that 'bottle ale' was becoming popular at the time. The explanation is probably that the two terms were already becoming interchangeable.

In 1703, the imposition by the Whig government of a heavy duty on French wines, in order to discourage support for the economy of France under the megalomaniac Louis XIV, caused strong ale of high quality to be served in decanters at table. Formal recognition having been thus accorded of its suitability for the elegant domestic scene, it was not long before flute glasses (q.v.) began to be considered the most appropriate to contain it, though it is possible that they had already been used for the purpose to some extent in the late 17th century. In this connection, it should be noted that the general assumption that flutes with short stems were dedicated exclusively to ale is not supported by conclusive evidence.

In the second half of the 18th century, a kind of rotund goblet or rummer (q.v.) began to be employed for the beverages under discussion, a fact which is deducible from the engraved decoration in the form of ears of barley and hops which had already appeared on many other glasses.

Air-twist (q.v.) as well as plain stems occurred, and in 1760 we hear of 'long enamelled ale glasses' which presumably meant flutes with opaque-twist (q.v.) stems.

Engraved ale flute, c. 1740

In the neo-classical phase associated with the name of Robert Adam in the last quarter of the 18th century, rummers were extensively used for malt liquor as for other beverages. Examples have been noted bearing, on the same glass, ornament in the form of hops, ears or sheaves of barley, and fruiting vines, indicative of the general utility of these popular vessels. Towards the end of the century, tall ale glasses with conical bowls might be cut or moulded with fluting (q.v.), while others with short or rudimentary stems appear from their thickness and limited elegance to have been intended mostly for use in taverns, though many were fashioned from glass of good quality.

In the early 19th century, many types of ale or beer glasses existed concurrently. These included the new kinds of rummers which appeared after 1800, various forms of the flute, and a novel variety with a flat-based, convex-sided bowl, tall in relation to its width, mounted on a short stem with a bladed or annular knop (q.v.) in the centre. The capacity was somewhat greater than that of the average flute, though it was not, of course, necessary to fill the glass to the brim. This type is often referred to in books on glass as a 'Georgian ale': a singularly imprecise term when we consider that strong ale had been drunk throughout the 18th century, and that the description 'Georgian' may be applied to anything made between 1714 and 1830.

Ale glass, c. 1810

Another variety, also with a convex-sided bowl, was narrower in relation to its height and should therefore be regarded as one of the many kinds of flute. It sometimes had an unusually thick foot like that of a firing glass or ship's glass (q.q.v.), and may, in fact, have been intended for use on board ship.

Many ale or beer glasses of the Regency period were exactly like contemporary wine glasses apart from the engraved hops and barley. This is hardly surprising in view of the fact that strong ale was as potent as wine and equally expensive; but one is left with the conviction that, since the bulk of our knowledge of the character of ale glasses is based on the evidence afforded by engraved or enamelled decoration, many other glasses of appropriate capacity without this decoration were used for strong ale or beer at the discretion of the owner. *See* also Cans.

Alemayne, John le: a commercial agent, evidently of German origin, who took orders for some of the window glass for St Stephen's Chapel, Westminster, and St George's Chapel, Windsor, between 1350 and 1356. This glass was made at Chiddingfold (q.v.) in Surrey.

Alloa: a glasshouse at Alloa in Clackmannanshire, Scotland, produced glass objects similar to those of Nailsea (q.v.) in the late Georgian period.

Altare: a glass-making centre near Genoa where, according to tradition, a number of glassworkers from Normandy and Picardy as well as Venice, settled in the 9th century, at a time when Rollo, the first Duke of Normandy, was wresting his duchy from the French Crown. Certain stylistic tendencies associated with Altare, such as a liberal use of applied work and gadroons – the latter being of Roman origin – were found in Liège in the 16th century, and may well have spread from there to England, where they were much in evidence from about 1660 to 1700, especially on vessels of the more important kind.

Amen glasses: *See* Jacobite glass.

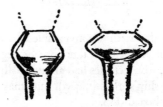

Angular knops

Angular knop: a knop on the stem of a glass, varying in depth and degree of projection and having a rounded triangular profile; occurring chiefly in the late 17th and early 18th centuries. *See* Stems.

Annealing: a process consisting essentially of heating finished glass artefacts to a high degree, followed by their controlled cooling through gradually reduced temperatures, in order to stabilize the metal (q.v.) by removing stresses. These stresses are set up when the glass is cooling after manufacture, owing to lack of uniformity in the rate at which the temperature falls throughout the mass. In a thick piece of glass, for example, the outside, which is in contact with the air, cools more quickly than the inside and will accordingly attempt to contract. The resultant stresses are permanent unless the glass is properly annealed, and simply await a critical frequency of vibration for cracking to occur. These matters were well understood even prior to the introduction of glass-of-lead by Ravenscroft (q.v.), but in general, insufficient attention was paid to them, and annealing chambers, which might be above or beside the furnaces, were inefficient owing to the difficulty of maintaining a proper degree of control. In about 1745, however, when the matter was discussed by the Royal Society, the tunnel leer (spelt 'lehr' in some books) was introduced from Germany, the word being a contraction of *leeres Ofen* – an empty oven. This consisted of a chamber along which finished glass objects moved slowly on iron pans until they reached the delivery-end, where they were cool enough to be handled. The tunnel leer, while still imperfect, probably brought about a significant reduction in wasters. Matters were greatly improved in 1778, when George Ensall of Stourbridge designed a leer in which the heat could be better controlled. His design was reputedly based on what would now be called 'industrial espionage', for it is said that he visited many glasshouses in Germany in order to acquire information, disguised as a travelling musician, though the story may well be apocryphal.

Annular knop: a knop in the form of a ring, possibly deriving from a similar formation on the stems of certain silver standing cups of the 16th century. This knop did not occur to any great extent until the early 19th century. *See* Stems.

Annulated knop

Annulated knop: a knop on a stemmed glass object, consisting of three, five, seven, or nine contiguous glass rings, with the central ring more protuberant than the others. Annulated knops were current in the early 18th century, and were usually accompanied by subsidiary formations of a less emphasized kind, such as slim inverted balusters (q.v.). *See* Stems.

Apple motifs: apple blossom, foliage and fruit began to be engraved on some glasses dedicated to cider between 1730 and 1740. This cider was of wine-quality, and was often served in expensive glasses.

Arch and rectangle design: a cutting design, much used on Waterford decanters and jugs in the late 18th and early 19th centuries, consisting of round-headed arches resting on short rectangles, both being filled with fine diamonds produced by making opposed incisions with a sharp-edged wheel. *See* Waterford.

Armorial engraving and enamelling: coats of arms were engraved on glass in diamond point in the 17th century, but this technique was superseded by wheel-engraving in the second quarter of the 18th century when the broader effects were preferred. After 1750, enamelling began to be required by those who could afford it, as the heraldic tinctures could be accurately rendered by this means, whereas engraved heraldry was of necessity in monochrome. *See* Beilby.

Audentior ibo: an engraved Latin inscription sometimes occurring on Jacobite glass (q.v.) which might be freely translated 'I shall advance more boldly'.

Ayckbower, J. D.: a Dublin glass-maker of the end of the 18th century. *See* Dublin.

B

Ball knop: a protuberance, on the stem of a drinking glass etc., which might be truly spherical or slightly compressed. One of the simplest kinds of knop, it had occurred in England as early as the 11th century on silver chalices and secular standing cups, and was used by Verzelini (q.v.) on glasses made in London in the late 16th century, when the

Ball knop

surface bore slight vertical gadroons (q.v.). It appeared as a major stem-feature in the late 17th century after the introduction of lead crystal, and its popularity may have been encouraged by a similar formation on contemporary legged furniture known as the Portuguese swell. In the early 18th century, it generally ceased to be employed as a dominant feature, but occurred frequently thereafter on a smaller scale and playing a subordinate role. *See* Stems.

Baluster: a classical architectural detail, occurring in multiple form in balustrades, which provided the inspiration for the stems (q.v.) of certain British glasses from the 17th century onward. The term is commonly extended to stem-formations which, while unlike architectural balus-ters, are of heavy construction and coeval with the earlier representatives of the style. These include Acorn, Angular, Drop, Ball, Double, Annulated, Ovoid, Mushroom and Cylinder knops (q.q.v.). *See* Inverted baluster and True baluster.

Balustroid: a modern term sometimes applied to the stems of certain glasses of light construction which began to be made in the first quarter of the 18th century, and which are of a character suggestive of the balusters. Some of them comprise actual balusters, either true or inverted, and include the so-called Kit-Cat glass (q.v.). But as these differ from the originals of the species only in their less robust proportions, they might be better described as 'light balusters': a term usually reserved, for no logical reason, for certain 18th-century glasses made at Newcastle upon Tyne (q.v.). An obsession with classification has even led some writers on glass to apply the term 'balustroid' to plain stems with small isolated knops, which bear no resemblance whatever to balusters. It is suggested that such stems should be more accurately referred to as 'plain stem with small basal knop' and so forth. If, despite its slimness, a stem actually looks like a baluster, it should surely be described as a light baluster. *See* Light balusters.

Barilla: the soda-charged ash of certain plants, growing on the sea shore or in salt-marshes, which provided one of the alkaline constituents of fused glass. Much barilla was exported through the Spanish port of Alicante to various destinations, and the English glass-maker, Sir Robert Mansell, is known to have obtained supplies in the first quarter of the 17th century. A similar product known as *roquetta* was exported from Egypt. The alkali was also sometimes extracted from the plant *Salicornia herbacea*, which is found in various places round the British coast, its familiar name being Glasswort.

Barrel-shaped decanter: a type of decanter first advertised in 1775, with a tall, narrow body like a contemporary wine-barrel, often cut with vertical fluting and spaced, annular incisions suggestive of staves and hoops. *See* Decanters.

Baskets: small glass baskets were made shortly after the middle of the 18th century, chiefly for suspension from the branches of centrepieces (q.v.). Others, possibly for trinkets, sweetmeats etc., were fashioned from coloured glass, some being of inferior workmanship. Large versions were used for fruit.

Batch: the mixed ingredients charged into the melting pot for fusion into glass. *See* Glass.

Beaker: one of the most ancient forms of drinking vessel and occurring in most cultures and many materials, the typical beaker had a flat base of variable diameter and a cylindrical body which widened upwards to the brim. Examples in glass have survived in Britain from the Anglo-Saxon era and date mostly from the 5th and 6th centuries. Although the majority were probably imported from the glass-making region between the Seine and the Rhine, where a flourishing industry was in being by the 2nd century, some were quite possibly made in England, where there was a certain amount of glass-making activity. In the Anglo-Saxon period they consisted chiefly of two types: the cone-beaker and the claw-beaker. The first, which was often over 26 cm

Claw-beaker and cone-beaker, 6th century

high, was in the form of a narrow, straight-sided cone slightly everted at the lip, often decorated in the upper third with multiple encircling glass threads, and in the lower two-thirds with narrow, vertical loops suggestive of hairpins. This thread ornament was trailed on while the vessel was hot. The flat base was too small for the beaker to be left standing on it. Despite the practical inconvenience arising from their instability, cone-beakers have an air of great elegance and refinement.

Claw-beakers are so named because the bodies, which varied in shape but were always tall in relation to their width, were embellished with hollow glass 'claws', often looking somewhat like elephants' trunks. They display a sort of barbaric attractiveness which evidently recommended itself to Anglo-Saxon taste, for they have been found in Britain in comparatively large numbers. There is no doubt also that they were valued and appreciated, for they owe their survival to the fact that they were often buried with their owners. It must be recognized, however, that both these kinds of beaker were British by adoption rather than origin.

Evidence of the existence of glass industries in England between c. 600 A.D. and the early 13th century is extremly scanty, though an Anglo-Saxon glasshouse was excavated some years ago at Glastonbury in Somerset and glass-making was undoubtedly carried on in North-East England at the same period. But as metal beakers, almost certainly including silver examples, appear with great frequency in English manuscript illustrations of the early 11th century, that is, before the Norman conquest, it is very likely that comparable but cruder vessels were made locally of glass, the raw materials of which had no intrinsic value.

Some evidence, of a literally fragmentary nature, indicates the production of glass drinking vessels before the end of the 14th century, but we have to wait until the late 16th century for sufficiently sound fragments from which a recognizable beaker may be synthesized. The form which emerges – making due allowance for the different characteristics of the media – was presumably inspired by contemporary silver beakers with expansive foot-rings, for the glass version widened upwards and was mounted on a broad, thick foot. A similar glass is often used in modern times for lager-beer.

Between 1667 and 1673, the Glass Sellers' Company of London were sending designs to Venice so that their supplier might know what was required for the English market, and these included a drawing of a squat beaker intended for strong beer. It seems probable that native beakers of this kind, of inferior workmanship, were already an established English type, for the design must have had some rational basis. In the 18th century, vessels of similar proportions were generally called 'tumblers' (q.v.), a misnomer which has clung to them ever since. In this connection, it should be noted that a tumbler, or tumbler-cup, was a short silver beaker with heavy, rounded base, introduced in the second quarter of the 17th century. It received its name because it rocked or 'tumbled' from side to side when knocked, instead of falling over, whereas glass vessels designated by the name have always been very stable.

The corrupt usage seems to have been already established in the reign of Charles II (1660–85), when real tumblers were still made in silver and must have been familiar to a great many people, for there was mention of 'brandij tumblers' in an order sent to Venice. These were short cylindrical beakers of stable design.

In a purely terminological sense, it could be said that the glass beaker practically disappeared from the scene at the beginning of the 18th century, at a time when the silver beaker had ceased to enjoy any fashionable esteem. But there is still some small tendency to apply the term to what might otherwise be called a tumbler, if it is mounted immediately on some kind of foot which is wider than the base of the actual receptacle.

Beer-jugs: glass jugs begin to survive in large numbers only from the last quarter of the 18th century, and were presumably used by their owners for anything they chose. They are described specifically as beer-jugs or ale-jugs only when they are engraved with hops and barley to indicate their primary purpose. The usual capacity was one quart, and they sometimes had cut or moulded comb-fluting (q.v.) round the lower part of the body. In glass-sellers' lists of the early 19th century, jugs of similar size, often with cut decoration, were usually described as water-jugs, though this fact would have been unlikely to deter an owner from using one for beer if he wished to do so. *See* Jugs.

Beilby: William Beilby (1740–1819) and his sister Mary (1749–97) are the most distinguished personalities in the history of the enamelled decoration of British glass, though it is only fair to add that there were many other competent practitioners of the art of whom we know nothing. Their father, who was born in 1706, was a successful silver-smith who worked in Durham, where there was no assay-office, and moved later to Newcastle upon Tyne which had its own town mark. William and Mary lived in Newcastle with their mother and brother Ralph: a silversmith and engraver who taught the latter art to the more celebrated Thomas Bewick.

In about 1762 they began to practise enamel-painting on glass, though it seems unlikely, in view of her age, that Mary's participation at this stage was on a very considerable scale. Their efforts, however, were evidently soon attended by a great deal of success, for Thomas

25

Bewick recorded that, in 1767, they enjoyed 'constant employment of enamel-painting on glass'.

The earliest work was probably of an heraldic nature, for this demanded painstaking application rather than artistic flair; but it was undoubtedly very good of its kind. Several examples have survived bearing the Royal arms, with all the tinctures accurately rendered, enclosed in rococo cartouches, and these were almost certainly designed to commemorate the birth of the Prince of Wales, the future George IV, in 1762. It may be safely assumed that this work was executed while the event was still topical.

The glasses selected for this and other heraldic embellishment were mostly large goblets of important aspect with bucket-shaped or ogee (q.v.) bowls, supported on various kinds of stems including opaque-twist and air-twist (q.q.v.). Some of the blazonry was carried out in white tin-oxide enamel instead of colour, and presumably cost the customer less. A certain amount in both colour and monochrome displayed heraldry of a fictitious nature, which probably owed its existence to inferiority complex on the part of merchants and others in Newcastle and the surrounding country.

Objects other than drinking glasses, such as bowls and decanters, were also enamelled, and the latter, in addition to the coats of arms which sometimes occurred, frequently bore painted representations of bottle tickets with the name of the contents. These bottle tickets were generally made of silver and were hung round the necks of decanters by thin chains; in the painted versions, the chains were often rendered in enamel in conventionalized form.

Apart from work of the more formal kind, which sometimes included gilding, the Beilbys soon began to execute designs of a more pictorial variety, such as landscapes, drinking scenes, sporting events, classical ruins and so forth, in addition to hops and barley, Masonic emblems, birds, flowers, butterflies, grapevines and vine-trails, fine detail such as leaf-veins being incised with a needle. A typical Beilby butterfly, either rising or alighting, occurred so frequently in addition to other designs of various kinds that it is often interpreted as a deliberate symbol of authorship. But whether this interpretation is correct or not, it is very easily recognizable and thus assists identification.

Some of the work was signed 'Beilby', which suggests that neither brother nor sister wished to monopolize the credit – an arrangement which probably operated more for the benefit of Mary than William – but in practice there is little difficulty in attribution on stylistic grounds.

One is also assisted by the nature of the white enamel, which displays a bluish, or occasionally pinkish, tinge.

After their mother died in 1778, the Beilbys left Newcastle, which had provided them with their glasses, and settled in Fifeshire, and it seems probable that they abandoned their work at the same time and lived on the fruits of their previous labours.

An examination of drawings on paper by William discloses the fact that, when he ventured outside his usual field of activity, his draughts-manship often left much to be desired. But despite the fact that he was in no sense a great artist, there is no doubt that his enamel-painting on glass has considerable charm which, combined with its comparative rarity, renders authentic specimens both desirable and valuable.

Belfast: in 1771, Benjamin Edwards of Bristol started a glass-making enterprise at Drunrea in Ireland, possibly because the Glass Excise Act of 1745 imposed no taxes on Irish glass, so that Ireland afforded op-portunities of manufacturing more cheaply than in Bristol. As the same Act prohibited the export from Ireland of any glass whatsoever, it may be assumed that Edwards hoped to make a commercial success of supplying local markets from Drunrea. It may also be assumed that he was disappointed in this hope, for in 1776, he transferred his operations to Belfast, where he began to manufacture all the usual items of domestic glass with the aid of an English cutter, much of it being unidentifiable. In this new situation he evidently prospered, and when the ban on the export of glass from Ireland was raised by the British Parliament in 1780, he began to advertise cut and plain decanters shortly after.

As might be expected, Belfast decanters showed a general similarity to those made at Bristol and elsewhere in Britain at the same time, and although the glasshouse continued in production into the second quarter of the 19th century, Edwards, and his son who succeeded him in 1812, continued to be inspired by the influence of Bristol and preserved a noticeable conservatism in design.

It is fortunate that we are able to identify some of the Belfast de-canters beyond doubt by the fact that they were marked underneath with the name of the factory. The mark consisted of letters arranged in a circle forming the legend 'B. Edwards Belfast'. This applied only to decanters which were mould-blown, the letters appearing in reverse in the bottom of the mould. The mould was useful for other reasons. First, it facilitated the production of objects of the same size and, secondly, it enabled comb-fluting (q.v.) to be imparted to the lower sides of the object by vertical ribs on the inside of the mould. This moulded comb-fluting had a soft, liquid appearance in comparison with cut fluting. The latter was executed with an abrasive wheel both on existing moulded work and on free-blown decanters which naturally bore no mark, but these may be readily identified as of Belfast origin by analogy with marked specimens.

From the commencement of the factory's operations to the beginning of the 19th century, these decanters were similar in proportion to the tapering decanters which had begun to be made in Britain in the late 1760s, but with slightly more curvature in the profile of the body. The pouring-lip projected only very slightly, and the stoppers were either flat vertical discs with bevelled or sliced edges, or kite-shaped with the edges treated in a similar manner and sometimes with cruciform incisions on each face.

The neck-rings (q.v.), which owed their presence less to cosmetic considerations than to the desirability of providing a firm grip, were two in number instead of the three commonly found elsewhere, and were of triangular profile, of a type which occurred frequently in Bristol.

Although, as mentioned earlier, Benjamin Edwards advertised 'cut and plain decanters', cut decoration was never extensive in Belfast and never competed for attention with the attractive shape. It consisted of little more than stars, built up from radiating incisions, vertical flutes occupying the upper half of the body beneath the lower neck-ring, three circuits of printies (q.v.) in the same position, and sometimes rather perfunctory sliced festoons looping round the widest part which were presumably inspired by the neo-classical swags which were a common element of the Adam style.

Shortly before 1800, a shorter decanter of modified shape appeared as an alternative to the existing type. The neck was lengthened at the expense of the rest and this, combined with the overall shortening, made it necessary to increase the width of the body in order to maintain the capacity. Decanters of the same shape were made in Bristol and Cork (q.v.), but those originating in the latter never had triangular neck-rings, while some of the typical Belfast details already mentioned, apart from marking, help to distinguish Edwards' decanters from those made in Bristol in a similar style.

In the last years of the 18th century, some vertical disc stoppers used at Belfast and many other places began to be embellished with moulded radial gadroons (q.v.) round a central depression, and this feature became especially popular after 1800.

Belfast decanter, c. 1790

Belfast glassware other than decanters cannot usually be distinguished from that made in other centres, though it seems probable that the volume of production was small in comparison with that of Waterford, Cork, and most British glasshouses. This very circumstance, however, imports a certain degree of rarity, and this, combined with high quality and pleasing design, makes a Belfast decanter a desirable acquisition.

The demise of the glasshouse in the 19th century was almost certainly due to the extension of the Glass Excise Act (q.v.) to Ireland in 1825, which deprived it of the advantages afforded by previous immunity from taxation.

Bellows: glass bellows, often in various colours, were among the trifles made at Nailsea (q.v.) and elsewhere from the last decade of the 18th century.

Bells: glass bells were made in the early 19th century, and were rung in glassworkers' processions. They were frequently coloured, but the clappers were of plain glass. There are many later reproductions.

Bell-shaped bowl: the bowl of a drinking glass, sweetmeat glass and so forth, with a rounded base and the sides expanding outward to the rim in a hollow curve. *See* Bowls of glasses.

Betrothal glass: a drinking glass given in celebration of a betrothal and bearing an appropriate engraved inscription often consisting of name, initials, true lovers' knots and sometimes a date. Examples have survived from the late 16th century.

Betts, Thomas: celebrated London glass seller who was well established in Bloomsbury by 1738. He was originally a 'glass-grinder', that is, he bevelled the edges of looking-glasses as had been done in London since the reign of Charles II, but soon became concerned with cut glass of all kinds, the work, in the early stages, being performed by a German or Bohemian cutter whose name was anglicized to Andrew Pawl. It was presumably from Pawl that Betts acquired the requisite finer techniques which enabled him to do the cutting himself, for after moving in about 1740 to 'The King's Arms Glass-Shopp, Opposite Pall-Mall, Charring Cross', he issued a trade card bearing the phrase 'He being the Real Workman for many Years'. This trade card listed the cut-glass objects which he was prepared to supply, and included cruets, casters, salts, lustres, desserts, punch-bowls, cream bowls, salvers, plates and dishes. It also made the claim that his productions were 'Cheaper & Better than hitherto has been done'. No mention was made of drinking glasses, but the presence of these, representing the largest category of all glass objects, must have been generally assumed, for surviving invoices leave no doubt that they formed a significant part of his sales together with decanters. He died in 1767. *See* Cut glass.

Bishopp, Hawley: partner to George Ravenscroft (q.v.) and who took over the management of the experimental glasshouse at Henley-on-Thames in 1676 and the Savoy glasshouse in London after Ravenscroft's death in 1681, under an 'Indenture of Agreement' with the Glass

Sellers' Company. By this time, technical problems which had plagued Ravenscroft had been largely overcome, and under Hawley Bishopp, English lead crystal attained general recognition.

Bladed knop

Bladed knop: a small protuberance of acute triangular profile on the stem of a glass object, sometimes comparatively sharp; common from about 1800. *See* Stems.

Blazes: a cutting design of the early 19th century. *See* Cut glass.

Blore Park: situated near Market Drayton in Shropshire, Blore Park became the site of glass-making activities in the last quarter of the 16th century, when craftsmen from Lorraine moved there from Buckholt in Hampshire where they had begun to encounter hostility on the part of native workers who probably resented their superior technique and greater commercial success. Some of their furnaces were excavated in 1931, and anglicized versions of their names appear in the registers of Eccleshall Parish Church, near Market Drayton, where several of them are referred to as being from 'Blower Parke', The settlement appears to have endured for about forty years.

Blowing tube: the blowing tube or blowing iron was invented in Syria in the 1st century B.C. No innovation of comparable importance in glass-making has been made since. It consisted of a metal tube, about 1.5 m long, which was dipped in the crucible of molten glass and twisted about until a sufficiently large 'gather' adhered to the end. This was then taken to a smooth slab of stone, or later of iron, and rolled on its surface in order to shape it, the rolling process being interrupted as necessary for the workman to raise the tube to his mouth and inflate the

31

glass with his breath. The paraison (q.v.) could be elongated by allowing it to droop downward or by swinging it round vertically. To enable the object to be finished, it was transferred to a pontil or punty (q.v.). *See* Mould-blown.

Bonnet glass: *See* Monteith (b).

Boot glass, c. 1800

Boot glasses: drinking glasses in the shape of high-legged boots, made in the second half of the 18th century and the early 19th century. They varied considerably in size and are curiosities rather than objects of beauty. They are sometimes called Bute glasses on account of a common supposition that they represented a practical lampoon on Lord Bute, Prime Minister from May 1762 to April 1763, who rendered himself obnoxious to the subjects of George III by introducing a tax on cider and negotiating the unpopular Treaty of Paris. This supposition is, however, almost certainly incorrect, for many similar glasses were made in Antwerp and Liège. Boot glasses have survived in large numbers.

Bottles: bottles of various kinds have been made of glass since about the middle of the 2nd millennium B.C., when the production of glass vessels commenced in the Eastern Mediterranean, and many types including apothecaries' phials began to be produced in Britain at least as early as the 14th century. The term 'bottle' is of extremely wide application, and to confine the matter within reasonable bounds, we shall concern ourselves in this section only with wine bottles, which began to emerge from English glasshouses in the early 17th century and followed a recognizable evolutionary pattern. They were all made of the dark green or brownish glass which is still used for the purpose, though some were almost black.

Many bore a device and initials on an applied circular pad, sometimes accompanied by a date, and these, which are now commonly known as 'serving-bottles', were used to convey wine from the cask to the table as well as for storing it, before decanters (q.v.) became widely current in the 18th century.

The earliest type had the general appearance of an Italian *fiasco* for Chianti, with a long neck and globular body, but with the base pushed in to form a 'kick' to enable it to stand upright. A narrow glass ring was applied round the top of the neck a short distance below the rim, the original purpose of which was to provide a purchase for the string that was bound over the waxed cloth or cork with which the bottle was sealed when used for storage rather than serving. This feature persisted well into the 18th century, and even after it lost its original function remained as a reinforcement.

Bottle, c. 1660   Bottle, c. 1680

In the next stage of evolution, which began shortly after the middle of the 17th century, overlapping the first phase and continuing until about 1685, the neck of the bottle became shorter. At the same time, the body lost its quasi-spherical form and narrowed inward towards the base just below the middle. An example of this kind is known bearing the head of King Charles II and the date 1661, presumably to commemorate the coronation.

From about 1680 until the second decade of the 18th century, the neck was shorter still, and the body assumed a shape which was practically an inversion of the previous type, being wide at the base and narrowing upwards in a smooth, convex curve so that it looked somewhat like a dome.

It will be noticed that all the foregoing had rounded profiles despite variations in total aspect. They are sometimes described as 'Shaft-and-globe, types one and two' and 'Dome-shaped'. The curvature in the profile made such bottles difficult to store on their sides in bins, so that they were frequently laid in sand or sawdust on the floor of the cellar. The object of binning is, of course, to keep the base of the cork in contact with the wine to prevent it from drying out and admitting air, which would bring about chemical changes in the wine.

Bottle, c. 1700   *Bottle, c. 1730*

The inconvenience arising from the shapes in question may have brought about the next modification, which involved the straightening of the sides, which sloped outward to the base, giving such a bottle the appearance of a mason's or sculptor's mallet. For this reason, the type is known as 'mallet-shaped', though the author has seen it described in a large provincial auction room by the meaningless term 'semi-squat'. The mallet-shaped bottle persisted up to the middle of the 18th century, but meanwhile, the sides of a great many had begun to be vertical from about 1735. This formation soon became dominant until, with the passage of time, the diameter was gradually reduced and the height increased, resulting in the appearance of a cylindrical bottle of more or less modern aspect in the last quarter of the 18th century.

Apart from ordinary wine bottles of circular section, many others were of square shape. It is not known precisely when the latter were first manufactured in Britain, but the shape had been common among mould-blown artefacts during the Roman occupation and had a history which began long before this. It is known that travelling canteens were made for journeys by coach in the first half of the 17th century, and almost certainly included square bottles, which were more easily packed and more secure than bottles of normal section. By the middle of the 18th century they were commonplace and their manufacture constantly increased.

Bottle, c. 1760   *Bottle, c. 1780*

It is difficult to decide whether many examples of the second half of the 18th century and first half of the 19th century should be considered as bottles or decanters, because contemporary descriptions varied. Those intended for travelling were often called case-bottles, while an advertisement of 1769 in the *London Evening Post* mentioned 'square decanters for public houses'; but there is no satisfactory way of distinguishing between them when case-bottles have become separated from their cases and are made of colourless flint glass. All are extremely difficult to date unless they bear cut motifs of a positive kind which enable them to be assigned to a particular period. (*See* Cut glass). They were sometimes engraved with the owner's monogram and might be partly gilt.

We must now give some consideration to a kind of bottle known as a 'flask'. From the early 18th century, the term had a special significance which is indicated by the alternative name 'wanded bottle', which meant that it was enclosed in wickerwork. Flasks were used for a number of different purposes where the contents were deemed especially worthy of protection, and these purposes included the storage of champagne, though ordinary bottles were sometimes employed for this wine instead. A picture by Sir Godfrey Kneller in the National Portrait Gallery, London, shows the Duke of Newcastle and the Earl of Lincoln. It appears to have been painted soon after the young duke succeeded to the title in 1711 and, indeed, both gentlemen might well be celebrating the occasion, for Newcastle is shown grasping a wicker-covered bottle, while Lincoln holds a glass containing a light-coloured wine which appears to have foam on its surface. (*See* Kit-Cat glass.)

Bowes, Sir Jerome (died 1616): on the retirement of Verzelini (q.v.) in 1592, Sir Jerome Bowes, erstwhile soldier and English Ambassador to Russia in 1583, purchased a twelve-year monopolistic patent to make glass vessels of all kinds in London, and commenced operations at a glasshouse in Broad Street. He was a courageous and energetic man. It is recorded that when he first appeared at the Russian court, he kept his hat on, and the furious Czar told him that unless he removed it forthwith, it would be nailed to his head. Bowes coolly replied that the Queen whom he represented did not 'bare her head to any prince living', and this so astonished the Czar that Bowes was permitted to remain covered without the assistance of nails. However, his boldness of approach, more becoming a soldier or a pirate than a businessman, caused some trouble among the workers at Broad Street, but the enterprise prospered notwithstanding. He became well liked by his fellow citizens to such a degree that, in 1597, 'the inhabitants of St. Ann, Blackfriars, built a fair warehouse under the isle' for his use, and also gave him £133. It may be safely assumed that his glass was of a similar kind to that of Verzelini. None has been identified beyond doubt, though it is probable that the 'Barbara Potter' glass, preserved in the Victoria and Albert Museum, London, came from his factory in Broad Street. It has a bell-shaped bowl – of a type which, in modified form, was destined to be popular in the 18th century – engraved in diamond point with decorative motifs including the name of the owner and the date 1602.

Bowes obtained an extension of his patent after its expiry in 1604, but his previous monopoly was no longer absolute. The eventual decline of his business may have been due both to difficulties arising from James I's decree of 1615 which banned the use of wood as an industrial fuel, and to illness which preceded his death. He was buried at Hackney Church on 28 March 1616. *See* Mansell.

Bowles, Benjamin: an important 18th century glass-maker whose manufactory was in Stony Street, Southwark, on the right bank of the Thames. He was well known for his 'opake' white glass, and in 1744, some 'composition glass', presumably consisting of a mixture of flint glass and tin oxide, was stolen from his warehouse. This was about the time when the opaque-twists began to appear in stemmed glass objects including drinking vessels, but Bowles' activities evidently extended far beyond manufactures of this kind, for it is recorded that 'The white glass of Mr Bowles' glasshouse in Southwark is frequently used for the grounds of enamel dial plates'.

Bowles, John (1640–1709) a London glass-maker, who carried on his business at the Ratcliff factory in Southwark. He made vessels in flint glass and also crown glass (q.q.v.) for windows, the latter being a branch of the trade in which he achieved some prominence. In 1678, he went into partnership with William Lillington. Many glass-makers of the period were applying seals to some of their productions, probably in imitation of Ravenscroft (q.v.), and a drinking glass preserved in the Northampton Museum is sealed on the stem with the figure of a female archer which is thought to indicate a Bowles and Lillington origin.

Bowls: in this section, we are concerned with independent bowls, rather than with parts of other objects to which the same term is applied (*See* Bowls of glasses). Glass bowls are simple to make and of wide utility, and their manufacture must have begun in the early years of glass-making. Examples imported from various parts of the Roman Empire as far apart as Alexandria and the Seine-Rhine region have been found in Britain, and it may be presumed that they were comparatively numerous until sea-borne trade became hazardous after the departure of the legions from Rome's most Northerly Province. Some of those found may possibly have been made in important centres like Colchester and Lincoln, but none has been identified.

As with other kinds of glass vessels, there is a long gap in the evidence coinciding with the medieval period, and although Venetian importations in the 15th and 16th centuries may well have provided a stimulus to later manufacture in Britain, survivors from among native bowls scarcely date from before the last quarter of the 17th century. One well-known example by Ravenscroft (q.v.) is the Butler-Buggin bowl in the Victoria and Albert Museum, London. Its period is deducible not only from the nature of the metal but also from engraved ornament which provides a clear provenance. This particular bowl has a smooth surface, but others might have applied vertical ribs, deriving, *via* Venice, from Roman gadroons (q.v.). An example of this kind, made by Ravenscroft, is in the Cecil Higgins Museum, Bedford. Horizontal trails sometimes occurred, and the rims of a great many were folded over to reduce the risk of chipping – a device frequently used in the 18th century.

In regard to 'ordinary' glass bowls, that is, bowls of an open shape similar to that of a bird's nest, the fact has to be faced that, as they were not made in sets like drinking glasses, their incidence has always been comparatively low and their ratio of survival lower still. Furthermore, as they have always preserved the same general form, with differences in detail which are not of much consequence, we are not assisted by any sort of stylistic evolution, so that assignment to any particular period must usually depend on superficial factors such as engraved, enamelled, or cut decoration, or on documentary evidence such as bills or inventories which provide a provenance but are seldom available.

During the 18th century, a glass bowl known as a Monteith (q.v.) enjoyed some degree of popularity, especially in the latter part, when it was probably used both as an alternative to the contemporary individual wine-glass cooler and as a punch-bowl. It outlasted its silver counterpart by many decades.

Apart from the foregoing, there were many types of bowl of less conventional design. Examples have survived from the late 17th century of a capacity appropriate for sugar, cream, or sweetmeats, and in regard to these and others it is seldom safe to dogmatize about their purpose.

The type in question stood on a low foot-ring and was surmounted by a cover with a decorative finial. The bodies of small bowls of the late 17th and early 18th centuries sometimes bore raised ornament, often wrythen (twisted). Their popularity declined later, probably as a result of the competition offered by small silver bowls which enjoyed greater prestige, but they never disappeared altogether. Others of similar proportions, but dedicated to specific purposes, such as finger bowls, are dealt with under their respective headings.

Covered bowls of various sizes on dish-like stands, and usually bearing cut decoration, began to appear after the middle of the 18th century, their intended use being a matter of conjecture. Some were small enough to have served as butter-dishes, others were large enough for punch-bowls, while certain specimens of intermediate capacity could have contained dessert concoctions or a generous quantity of sweetmeats such as orange-chips. The bowl itself might have a flexed

Covered bowl and stand, c. 1765

outline widening towards the top, with a sharply bevelled rim cut into double cymas, the same treatment being applied to the edge of the stand. The base of the bowl and stand were often cut in a carefully executed star design, while the top of the cover and the finial with which it was crowned were embellished with shallow, wheel-cut facets.

The star-cutting on the bottom of the bowl and the stand was often precisely similar to that found on the walls of rectangular glass tea-caddies of the 1770s. The cover almost invariably fitted inside the rim of the bowl, whether the edge of the latter was cut or plain.

Double cyma

All the bowls which have been discussed hitherto stood on their own bases, but many others, with or without covers, were raised on stems and feet from quite early in the 18th century. Those which had the proportions and size of goblets are considered under Sweetmeat glasses, though it must be recognized that there is a good deal of overlapping. Some standing bowls, as we shall call them, of the first half of the 18th century, might be as much as 27 cm high, and had covers, knopped stems, domed feet and ribbed or wrythen surfaces, the bowl being frequently about 18 cm in diameter. Such a standing bowl was, in fact, like an outsize ecclesiastical ciborium made of glass. Although survivors are rare, the same type continued through the usual phases of stem-treatment and included knopped, Silesian, air-twist, opaque-twist, and cut or moulded stems, the last often accompanied by cut bowls and covers.

Standing bowl, Irish, c. 1790

During the neo-classical phase, in the last quarter of the 18th century, large open standing bowls became especially prevalent, many of the heavier examples being made in Ireland, which was immune from the taxation imposed by the Glass Excise Act of 1745. Typically, the actual receptacle had the edge turned over to form a deep flange, and might be circular or oval. Both the flange and the outside of the bowl beneath it were mostly decorated with shallow cutting, which broke up transmitted light in an agreeable manner without impairing the transparency. Stems were usually knopped, while the feet, which were generally moulded, might be circular, lobed round the edge, lozenge-shaped, or square, the last two often being surmounted by a hollow dome with the sort of sharp, radial prisms or flutes underneath which were frequently found on contemporary rummers, salt-cellars and so forth, and to which the descriptive term 'lemon-squeezer' has been applied in modern times. Bowls of this kind are usually called fruit bowls or salad bowls, though it is unlikely that their use would have been restricted in any way. Like large bowls of conventional type, their production continued into the 19th century with cut decoration appropriate to the period. *See* Cut glass.

Bowls of glasses: the bowl of a glass is the receptacle which holds the wine or other liquid which is poured into it and, in this section, we shall devote our attention to the bowls of stemmed drinking glasses. Sweetmeat glasses are dealt with separately.

Round funnel bowl

ROUND FUNNEL: it is not practicable to begin our survey before the time of Verzelini (q.v.), who received a patent from Queen Elizabeth I to make 'Venice glasses' in England. Despite his Venetian origin, he was strongly influenced by the predilections of the English market. Several of his bowls were of round-funnel type, others were curved round funnels with a profile in the form of a catenary curve, borrowed, apparently, from contemporary English silver standing cups.

BELL SHAPE: a bell-shaped bowl, on a glass probably made at the factory of Sir Jerome Bowes (q.v.), has survived from the beginning of the 17th century, and was a type which was used in the 18th century and later.

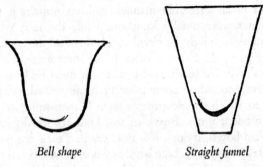

Bell shape   *Straight funnel*

STRAIGHT FUNNEL: even before the introduction of glass-of-lead by Ravenscroft (q.v.) in 1675, the straight funnel or conical bowl was already in existence with glasses made of soda or potash metal, so that by the time a truly national style began to emerge in the last quarter of the 17th century, many of the subsequent bowl-forms were already well established. One version of the straight funnel at this period curved slightly inward towards the rim, but was not widely used.

POINTED ROUND FUNNEL: in the early 18th century, the pointed round funnel was a feature of various glasses including the Kit-Cat (q.v.).

 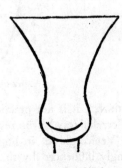

Pointed round funnel   *Waisted bell*

WAISTED BELL: at the same time, the waisted bell began to become popular and consisted of the existing bell-shape modified by the presence of a 'waist', that is, a zone between the rim and the base which was narrower than either. The globular base of such a bowl consisted, in the earlier examples, of solid glass, sometimes containing a 'tear' of air. The lowest part of this bowl and the round funnel was sometimes constricted to form a cyst (q.v.).

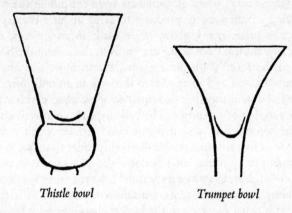

Thistle bowl   *Trumpet bowl*

THISTLE BOWL: a type related to the above is usually described as a thistle bowl. It was somewhat similar to the waisted bell, but the diverging sides, above the solid ball of glass which formed the base, were straight instead of concave. An uncommon derivative, confined to the early years of the 18th century, had a base which was manipulated into something approaching the shape of an acorn, and almost invariably rested on a stem which was surmounted by a mushroom knop (q.v.). It was no doubt inspired by the acorn knop (q.v.) but should be distinguished from it, as the latter was purely a stemformation. This might sound a trifle confusing, but there is seldom any difficulty in practice, as the position of the weld between the top of the stem and the base of the bowl in such a glass is usually quite obvious. *See* Thistle dram.

TRUMPET BOWL: trumpet-shaped bowls were common in Venetian and Venetian-inspired glasses of the 16th and 17th centuries, but did not appear in Britain in lead crystal until after 1700. In the early stages, among glasses of heavy construction, they seem to have been confined chiefly to examples of small capacity intended to contain the highly spirituous cordials (q.v.) which were a contemporary equivalent of modern liqueurs. The sides were concave like those of the bell, but had flat, instead of rounded, bases. In the reign of Queen Anne (1702–14), when lighter glasses began to be manufactured, the trumpet bowl figured on a great many, and might occur above a miniature ball knop, a slim inverted baluster, or a true baluster (q.q.v.) of equally slight proportions which was in one piece with the bowl. In the second decade of the 18th century, when glass-makers were expanding their market by reducing manufacturing processes to bring about a corresponding reduction in price, many glasses were made in two pieces, the un-knopped, cylindrical stem being drawn from the base of the bowl and welded to the foot. With these glasses, the trumpet was one of the earlier bowl-forms, and merged into the stem in an unbroken line, so that bowl and stem together presented an appearance which was truly analogous to that of a trumpet. The bell-shape also occurred on glasses of similar construction, and it is not quite certain which came first, though the drawn trumpet was undoubtedly easier to make. A slightly later contemporary of the latter had straight, instead of concave, sides. This is known either as a DRAWN STRAIGHT FUNNEL or simply as STRAIGHT-SIDED, though the second term is insufficiently precise, as it could be applied with equal accuracy to the bucket-shaped bowl which will be considered later.

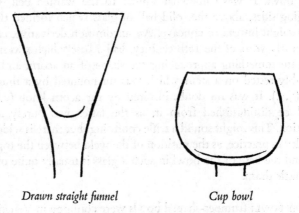

Drawn straight funnel   *Cup bowl*

CUP BOWL: this needs only passing mention. It was a rare type which came on the scene in the first quarter of the 18th century and presumably derived from the roemer (q.v.). It was usually mounted on a plain stem but was sometimes found later with an incised twist (q.v.). Some amateurs of old glass associate it exclusively with the service of mead, though no satisfactory evidence has ever been adduced in support of this notion. It occurred occasionally on beer-goblets.

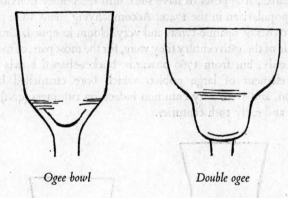

Ogee bowl   *Double ogee*

OGEE BOWL: this began to become popular in about 1740. The name is slightly unfortunate in view of the fact that an ogee, strictly speaking, is a low S-curve, whereas the bowl under discussion makes an angular change of direction in the lower part. It occurred mostly on wine glasses of average capacity which initially had plain cylindrical stems, but persisted into the second half of the 18th century often with stems of air-twist, opaque-twist, or faceted type (q.q.v.). Shortly before 1750, these bowls might have rather self-effacing moulded fluting (q.v.) round the lower half, or some other kind of impressed ornament. They were occasionally polygonal.

DOUBLE OGEE: this occurred at about the same time as the above on drinking glasses, though it had been known in a wider version on sweet-meat glasses soon after 1700. The sides of this bowl curved suddenly outwards about half-way up before rising more or less vertically. It was never particularly popular, but was restored to favour to some extent after 1800 when it sometimes appeared on rummers.

WAISTED OGEE: this was used in the second half of the 18th century, but its incidence was trifling.

BUCKET: the bucket-shaped bowl already alluded to was found on a type of silver standing cup, in the reign of Charles I (1625–49), which was probably inspired originally by the beaker. A glass variant in soda metal has survived from the Mansell (q.v.) period, and the shape occurred again in a narrower version on designs for glasses sent from London to Morelli (q.v.) of Venice in the time of Charles II (1660–85); but thereafter, it appears to have sunk into temporary oblivion until it was repopularized in the 1740s. Accompanying stems were plain or with air-twists or opaque-twists and very seldom knopped. Until after the middle of the 18th century they were, for the most part, of moderate capacity only, but from 1760 onwards, bucket-shaped bowls were a popular element of large goblets which bore enamelled heraldic decoration, and were very common indeed on rummers (q.v.) of the late 18th and early 19th centuries.

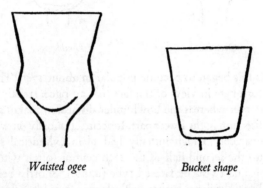

Waisted ogee   *Bucket shape*

WAISTED BUCKET: this began to furnish a variation on the same theme soon after the introduction of the bucket-shape.

OVOID: shortly before 1750, the ovoid bowl began to rival the ogee and easily surpassed it within a few years, being particularly common

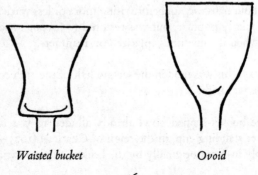

Waisted bucket   *Ovoid*

on cut glasses up to the end of the century. It varied somewhat in its proportions, and might be tall and narrow in the form of a flute glass (q.v.), particularly after 1770, or short and squat, with further variations between these two extremes. Some of the shorter examples approach the cup-shape, but with a slightly less sudden transition from bowl to stem due to the two-piece construction of the glass.

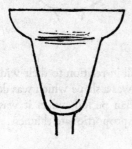
Saucer-topped round funnel

Pan-topped round funnel

SAUCER-TOPPED ROUND FUNNEL: a somewhat *outré* type which appeared in the middle years of the 18th century, the meaning of the term being self-evident.

PAN-TOPPED ROUND FUNNEL: this came on the scene at the same time as the above, but differed from it in that the broader process at the top was deeper and had almost vertical sides. It sometimes looked rather like a double ogee. Both this type and the one before were rare and neither was particularly pleasing.

FLANGED OR LIPPED ROUND FUNNEL: this was rarer still, and consisted of a round-funnel bowl with an emphatically everted rim, though the term is sometimes applied to what is really nothing more than a true bell. The latter attained more popularity after 1800, when it was usually cut with vertical fluting and mounted on a true or inverted baluster stem.

U-SHAPE: this occurred sparsely in the late 18th century and was seldom attractive except when in the form of a large serving-rummer (q.v.), when it was redeemed from banality by the sheer quantity of crystal glass. It began to exert more appeal to contemporary taste after 1820, when it was found in many sizes from small dram glasses to large

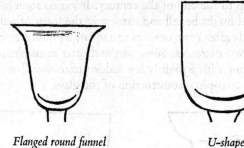

Flanged round funnel   *U-shape*

rummers which were comparatively tall in relation to their width and might have plain or facet-cut stems. It was a shape which was destined to be especially popular in the Victorian period, when it was often coloured and mounted on a stem of disproportionate thinness.

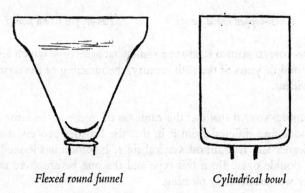

Flexed round funnel   *Cylindrical bowl*

FLEXED FUNNEL: after 1800, a few new shapes were introduced. These included a rummer-bowl which consisted of a very expansive round funnel or straight funnel which suddenly broadened out a short distance below the rim before rising vertically. It may have derived from the pan-topped round funnel mentioned above, but its total aspect was quite different.

CYLINDRICAL BOWL: a further recruit to the rummers of the same period, the cylindrical bowl differed from the U-shape in having a flat base. The stem was usually plain. It was certainly improved by the presence of a small knop, but these were mostly cheap utility glasses which were made as uncomplicated as possible to keep the price down.

BUCKET-AND-CYLINDER: this, the only other important newcomer during the Regency, occurred on what is often unsatisfactorily described as a 'Georgian ale': a term of excessively wide application. It consisted of a bucket-shape which suddenly changed direction half-way

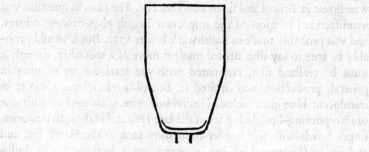

Bucket-and-cylinder

up and rose vertically. A basically similar shape of squatter proportions was found on a few wine glasses. The short stems of both types were usually embellished with a small centrally-placed knop in the form of a ring, though a bladed knop (q.v.) was sometimes used as an alternative.

Bristol: it seems probable that there was a glasshouse in Bristol as early as 1625, but the first satisfactory record relates to one which was founded in 1651 by a member of the Dagnia family (q.v.). Lead crystal was introduced in about 1690, and by 1696 there were three factories producing drinking glasses and other objects in what came to be called flint glass (q.v.). London remained the centre of fashion and manufactured the best glass in Britain for many years; but there is abundant evidence that the Bristol industry was in a flourishing state in the second quarter of the 18th century. In 1738, the Prince and Princess of Wales paid an official visit to the town, and the glass-workers, as part of the general festivities, mounted an ambitious display which betokened their importance in the local economy.

The industry continued to prosper throughout the 18th century, but was almost a spent force by the middle of the century following, the decline having begun during the Regency. In its heyday, it produced colourless flint glass of superb quality in addition to the coloured and opaque white glass with which it is now chiefly associated. Many people are under the impression that blue glass was an exclusive prerogative of Bristol in the Georgian era, but this impression is fallacious. It arises from the fact that the Saxon smalt, a vitreous frit coloured with cobalt, which produced the rich blue tint in glass of which it formed an ingredient, was obtainable at a certain period from the importer's warehouse in Bristol and from nowhere else. The glass in question was manufactured in most of the important British glass-making centres, and was probably made in Southwark before 1730. But it would probably be true to say that Bristol made it more of a speciality, though it must be realized that, compared with the total output of glass in general, production was limited in Bristol as elsewhere. Objects in translucent blue glass included individual wine-glass coolers with one or two pouring-lips, dating from the late 18th and early 19th centuries, finger bowls with gilt border-decoration such as the Greek fret and anthemion (honeysuckle), jars, canisters, vases, beakers, basins, bulb-glasses, mugs, rummers and so forth, and, perhaps more characteristic than any other, decanters (q.v.), either square or orthodox, bearing gilt labels in the form of imitation bottle tickets with the names of the contents. This embellishment derived from the silver bottle tickets which first appeared in the second quarter of the 18th century, and were hung round the necks of decanters by thin chains. In the gilt versions, the chains were often indicated in conventionalized form. Shouldered and tapering decanters were the chief variants, and bore either actual neck-rings of triangular or square shape, like those used in Belfast and Cork respectively but which originated in Bristol, or gilt encircling lines occupying the same position on the neck. Blue decanters for spirits were sometimes made in sets of three, labelled typically Gin, Rum and Brandy, and these were often accommodated in the retaining-rings of what looked like outsize cruet-stands, made of painted base metal.

From the time of the opening of the war with revolutionary France in 1793, supplies of smalt from Saxony became unobtainable, so that from the early years of the 19th century a less satisfactory artificial substitute was used. Four years or so after Waterloo, however, genuine smalt again became procurable, and the finest blue glass in which it was used came to be called 'King's blue', in recognition of George IV's delight at being presented with some as a coronation present in 1821.

In connection with two forms of decorative technique, Bristol blue glass must be considered a failure. These techniques were air-twists and cutting, which were suitable only for glass which was colourless or of light tone. The darkness of the blue rendered both almost entirely ineffectual. *See* Edkins and Jacobs.

Britannia glasses: glasses engraved with a figure of Britannia, made for various patriotic clubs during the Seven Years' War against France from 1757 to 1763. They were often of large size. Other glasses of the same period sometimes bore engraved portraits of Friedrich II of Prussia.

Broad glass: an archaic name for glass sheets formed by shaping the blown mass into a cylinder, splitting it and unrolling it. *See* Crown glass.

Broad Street glasshouse: one of the manufactories under the control of Sir Robert Mansell (q.v.) in the early 17th century, previously directed by Sir Jerome Bowes (q.v.).

Brunswick star

Brunswick star: a cutting design in use from about 1820 consisting, typically, of a twelve-pointed star with each point joined by a straight incision to the apex of the fifth point away from it. A small 'circle' formed the centre of the design.

Bucket-shaped bowl: a type of bowl in a shape suggestive of a bucket found on certain drinking glasses. *See* Bowls of glasses.

Buckholt: a glasshouse, manned by workers from Lorraine, existed at Buckholt in Hampshire in the last quarter of the 16th century.

Buckingham, Duke of (1628–87): George Villiers, second Duke of Buckingham, obtained patents for glass-making from Charles II in the names of several agents. He himself knew nothing of the craft, but allowed his finance and connections to be used by various practical men who did. His first glasshouse was in Charterhouse Yard, followed by others at Greenwich and Vauxhall, mirrors being made at the last-named. In 1664, Buckingham managed to have a ban placed on the import of looking-glasses from abroad, but this was revoked four years later because demand exceeded the domestic supply. Nevertheless, the productions of his glasshouses were esteemed at the period, John Evelyn the diarist stating that, at Greenwich, 'glasse was blown of finer mettal than that of Murano'. He also recorded that, in the Vauxhall glasshouse, were made 'looking-glasses far larger and better than any that come from Venice'. We cannot be altogether certain that these statements were not slightly exaggerated, but Evelyn, though something of a prig, was a highly intelligent man.

Bugles: beads made of dark-green or black glass, apparently first made in the late 16th century in East Sussex. *See* Camden, William.

Bulb glass, c. 1800

Bulb glasses: upward-tapering vases with a broad pan-shaped process at the top, used for the water-culture of hyacinths from the late 17th century; sometimes made of blue glass from the late 18th century or decorated with cutting.

Bute glasses: *See* Boot glasses.

Buttons: small spherical knops; the term occurs in the forms 'olive buttons' and 'wrought buttons', the latter being ribbed or otherwise decorated.

C

Camden, William (1551–1623): herald, historian and antiquary, wrote concerning Sussex industries in his *Britannia* (1586), 'neither does this county want glasshouses, but the glass (by reason of the matter or making I know not which) is not so transparent and clear and therefore is only used by the ordinary sort of people'.

Candelabra or table chandeliers: a candelabrum consists essentially of a candlestick, either actual or ostensible, with attached branches terminating in sockets. Examples in glass have survived from the end of the 17th century, but all are comparatively rare. *See* Candlesticks.

Candlesticks: glass candlesticks were known in Britain before the discovery of lead crystal in 1675, for it is recorded that, in 1671, eight pairs of various sizes were imported from the Continent for the use of the Duke of Monmouth. It seems probable, however, that none was made in Britain until after Ravenscroft (q.v.) had received general approval for his new metal. Thereafter, they provided an alternative for their counterparts in silver on the tables of the wealthy, and their production increased in the 18th century.

Candlestick, c. 1685

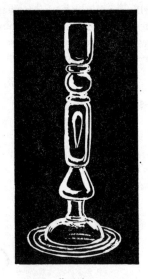

Candlestick, c. 1700

Candlestick, c. 1710

Candlestick, c. 1720,
Silesian stem

Some of the stem-features found on contemporary drinking glasses occurred also on candlesticks and tapersticks, which is not surprising when it is realized that these features had already appeared on brass candlesticks and silver standing cups long before they formed part of

Candlestick, c. 1740, air-twist stem

the glass-maker's repertoire. The general aspect of the two kinds of stem was, however, quite dissimilar, partly because drinking glasses were shorter and therefore accommodated fewer knops, partly because candlesticks retained earlier formations after they had ceased to be fashionable on the stems of drinking vessels. Analogies between the two cannot accordingly be pursued very far, but nevertheless, the same sequence was broadly followed. (*See* Stems.)

The earliest survivors have stems in the 'baluster' (q.v.) style, and include such elements as drop knops, annulated knops, and so forth, but these types are distinctly rare. When the Silesian (q.v.) stem was introduced in about 1714, it was resorted to with great enthusiasm by makers of candlesticks, who sometimes used it upside-down, that is, widening towards the bottom: a variant which was practically unknown on drinking glasses. Air-twists and opaque-twists (q.q.v.) were also found, though the incidence of the second was extremely low. This may well have been due to the fact that cutting began to be used to decorate glass candlesticks from shortly after 1740, and the refractive brilliance of cut crystal under candlelight must have created an effect of scintillation which an opaque-twist would have been wholly unable to rival.

Shortly after the time of their introduction, the majority of glass candlesticks had circular, domed feet, occasionally terraced, but during the neo-classical phase in the last quarter of the 18th century, feet were often square, as on some contemporary rummers (q.v.) and many silver

Cut candlestick, c. 1750   *Candlestick, c. 1775*

objects, while the stem of such a candlestick might embody a protuberance in the form of a classical urn. Although most were in colourless, transparent glass, some were made at Bristol and elsewhere in blue metal in the second half of the 18th century, and also in opaque white in imitation of porcelain, painted in enamel colours. These continued to be produced in the 19th century, often with decoration of an Oriental character.

In the late 18th and early 19th centuries, candlesticks were sometimes made with glass lustres hanging from the edge of the drip-pan. After 1800, the actual stem, partly concealed behind these pendants, was usually embellished with contemporary cut patterns such as relief diamonds and prismatic cutting (q.q.v.).

56

Cans or mugs: a can or mug, of whatever material such as pottery, pewter, silver, or glass, is a drinking vessel with a single handle and without a lid, now often miscalled a tankard (q.v.) through popular ignorance. Early surviving British examples in lead crystal, dating from the time of George Ravenscroft (q.v.), closely followed contemporary silver types, which had globular bodies and short cylindrical necks, their shape deriving from 16th-century vessels of a similar kind in salt-glazed stoneware. An early form of hyaloplastic embellishment, inspired at some distance by Imperial Roman taste *via* Venice, consisted of vertical gadroon-like ribs, either free or separated by shallow flutes, rising from the base and extending about a third of the way up the body.

Can or mug, c. 1680

This ornament, together with basal fluting, remained popular throughout the 18th century and is therefore of little assistance in dating. The same could be said, though to a less extent, of a kind of basal surface decoration which Ravenscroft called 'nipt diamond waies' (q.v.). This reticulated pattern, suggestive of chicken-wire, was also of Roman origin and reached Britain from Venice like the gadroons mentioned above. Far from being confined to the early years of lead crystal, it has been seen by the author on a cylindrical glass can which is known, by unimpeachable evidence, to have been made at Newcastle upon Tyne in the late 18th century.

The two chief shapes, cylinders and balusters, also enjoyed an endur-ing popularity. The first had been used for silver mugs from about 1685, the second from the last years of the 17th century. Another silver detail was a narrow moulded girdle running round the body, and this occurred from time to time on glass cans. All these features were current in glass until the early 19th century.

It will be realized from the foregoing facts that, since we are not provided with a tidy evolution of forms and ornament, dogmatic assertions as to dates of origin must generally be based on faith rather

Can or mug, 18th century

than evidence, unless assistance is afforded adventitiously by engraved or other surface ornament. Mugs, unfortunately, were decorated with cutting less frequently than other kinds of glassware. The colour of the metal is sometimes helpful, but can never be regarded as conclusive.

Carafes (Arabic *Gharrajah*): carafes, known also at various times as carrosts and crafts, which were used for wine or water, were made by Ravenscroft (q.v.) in the late 17th century and derived very clearly, though not necessarily immediately, from Roman examples of the 1st and 2nd centuries. They were tall and narrow, and tapered upwards to the upper fifth or sixth where they began to widen towards the brim. Similar carafes are sometimes seen in restaurants at the present day. In the 18th century, they followed the design of contemporary decanters, but with an everted pouring-lip and no stopper. Most survivors are from the early 19th century and later, when they were of globular form, with or without neck-rings, and mostly cut with fluting (q.v.).

In an advertisement of 1829 they were described as 'water bottles'. A tumbler was usually inverted over the mouth.

Carafe, c. 1810

Carré, Jean: an important Burgundian glass-maker who came to England from Antwerp in 1567, and set up a glasshouse in London with the object of producing, *inter alia*, 'all sorts of crystal drinking glasses like those of Venice'. He also made window-glass at Alfold in Sussex (*See:* Camden) with the aid of craftsmen from Lorraine, some of whose names, anglicized in various ways, have come down to us. Thus Houx became 'Hoe', Thisac 'Tyzack', Thiétry 'Tittery', and Hennezel 'Henzey', 'Ensell' or 'Ensall'. When the window-glass enterprise failed on Carré's death in 1572, these men departed to various places and helped to spread a knowledge of their techniques over a wider field. Perhaps Carré's chief claim to importance in British glass-history lies in the fact that, among a number of Venetian craftsmen brought in for the London operations, was Giacomo (Jacopo) Verzelini (q.v.).

Cased or overlay glass: this was introduced into Britain by travellers in Bohemia in the early 19th century, but does not appear to have been produced by British glass-makers until about 1830. Production increased considerably in the Victorian era, especially after the abolition of the tax on glass in 1845. It consisted typically of colourless glass with layers of coloured metal, from two to five, applied over it. Patterns were made by cutting through these layers so that contrasting hues were visible at the bases or edges of the incisions. Among the most typical of the earlier British items were tall decanters cased in ruby glass, emanating chiefly from the Midlands. Round the lower half of the body and from the shoulders to the top of the neck, were broad, cut flutes sometimes showing thin lines of ruby glass which remained on the dividing ridges. The upper half of the body retained much of its coloured casing, which was often engraved through to the underlying surface with fruiting vines. A cheaper alternative was provided later by flashed glass, the thin, coloured layers being applied by dipping.

Casters: casters for pepper and other spices and sometimes for sugar were made of glass as an alternative to silver from the mid-18th century, and were provided with pierced silver covers. They were mostly in cut glass of all the successive styles, and their dates can usually be determined by an examination of the hall marks on the silver.

Caudle cup: *See* Posset pot or caudle cup.

Celery vases: these vessels, which were produced on a fairly large scale in the second half of the 18th century, when cut decoration was fashionable, were always of similar proportions, though there were minor variations in overall shape. A typical celery vase had a receptacle which was tall in relation to its width and wider at the brim than at the base. This was mounted on a short stem which might be knopped or plain, while the foot might be square after about 1775. Cut decoration followed the normal pattern of evolution (*See* Cut glass) and became more plethoric after 1800. In the second decade of the 19th century, rims were frequently dentated and fan-cut: a form of treatment which persisted into the early Victorian period.

Centrepieces: silver centrepieces began to be made in the first quarter of the 18th century, but glass-makers were not inspired to emulation until about 1740. Early examples consisted, typically, of a standing bowl mounted on a tall stem, to which were attached curved branches from the ends of which glass baskets were suspended by their arching handles. Cut decoration varied in quantity but was a common feature. In the second half of the 18th century, there might be two sets of branches, the lower and larger ones being held in metal sockets. Styles underwent the usual changes in details found with other glassware, with part of the stem shaped like an urn in the late 18th century and often with a heavy square foot in the prevailing neo-classical idiom. Small cut lustres were sometimes attached to appropriate parts and candle-sconces were occasionally fitted, so that such a centrepiece was a kind of modified candelabrum.

As in the case of their silver counterparts, glass centrepieces began to be called *epergnes* after 1750. This French-sounding term was, however, invented in England and did not occur in the French language. It is possible that some influential British aesthete with a taste for the exotic formed the term from the word *épargne* – an economy or saving – the idea presumably being that it saved space to have the various utensils attached to a single object rather than spread round the table.

Celery vase, c. 1815

Chair: a wooden bench with parallel, horizontal arms, on which the 'gaffer', or head of a glass-making team, is seated to finish an artefact. The chair is less for his comfort than to enable him to do the job. The blowing-tube or pontil (q.q.v.) is placed across the arms and rolled along until shaping and trimming are completed, the rotary motion not only assisting the development of the desired form, but also preventing the glass, which is still in a plastic state, from collapsing under its own weight.

The word 'chair' or 'shop' is also used to denote the team of workers involved in any particular operation.

Chalices: glass chalices were occasionally made for liturgical use, especially after the Reformation, but were never anything but uncommon, as they offended ecclesiastical susceptibilities and were inconveniently fragile. Examples are known with silver foil sandwiched between two layers of glass.

Champagne decanters: *See* Ice decanters.

Champagne glasses: sparkling champagne was introduced to London society in 1670 by the Chevalier de St Evremond, an exile from the France of Louis XIV. Charles II gave him a pension of £300 a year and justified it, with typical dry humour, by appointing him Governor of Duck Island in St James's Park. From this time until about 1830, no special sort of glass appears to have been dedicated exclusively to champagne.

Flute glasses (q.v.) of fine metal were used for the wine as well as for other beverages including strong ale and cider of wine-quality, so that a probable association can be deduced only when such glasses are engraved with vines as opposed to hops and barley or motifs connected with apples, and even they would have been appropriate for other white wines such as Rhenish or Canary. The last-named was undoubtedly drunk from flutes in the 17th century, as contemporary literary references attest.

In the second half of the 18th century, allusions occurred not only to 'champain flutes' but also to 'egg champagnes'. The first were probably high-quality cut glasses, so that the expensive nature of the vessel was consonant with that of the wine. The second must have been goblets of appropriate capacity with ovoid bowls (q.v.), and were doubtless also embellished with cutting to enhance their apparant suitability.

Some writers on glass have expressed the view, with some dog-matism, that certain stemmed vessels of heavy construction with wide, capacious bowls were restricted to the service of champagne, but it must be pointed out that this notion is wholly unsupported by evidence. The glasses in question were almost certainly dessert utensils (*See* Sweetmeat glasses).

The kind of common conventional champagne glass with a bowl approaching a hemisphere in shape, was noticed by Disraeli in 1832 as something new, and it seems unlikely that it would not have come to his attention if it had been current for very long. With its wide, shallow bowl, which permits the maximum dispersal of carbon dioxide, it is probably the least suitable glass imaginable for a sparkling wine. Flutes, however, are still used in many parts of Europe for champagne, and to some extent in Britain.

Chandeliers: pendant light-fittings consisting of a central shaft to which multiple branches with candle-sockets were attached, derived from the wooden candle-beam of the medieval period. In the 17th century, they were common all over Europe and were usually in brass, but glass chandeliers were made in Venice at the same time and were exported to other countries. They may well have been produced in London in the last quarter of the 17th century, but the first reference to their sale occurred in the *London Gazette* in 1714 and related to John Gumley. He was mentioned as a furniture merchant in 1694, but was a famous manufacturer of looking-glasses in the reigns of Queen Anne (1702–14) and George I (1714–27) and official purveyor to the latter sovereign.

Advertisements for chandeliers became more frequent in the second quarter of the 18th century under the name of 'lustres', a term which had been reserved earlier for the hanging crystal drops with which they were decorated. In 1739, for example, Jerom(e) Johnson (q.v.) declared in a notice in the *Daily Post*, 'There is likewise to be sold cheap, the most magnificent Lustre that ever was made in England'.

Early English glass chandeliers were evidently modelled on their precursors in brass and were of uncluttered appearance, comprising a vertical shaft with bold, globular protuberances, and recurved branches attached to the lowest of the large mouldings. Cut decoration was shallow and was confined to the central shaft. In the 1740s, however, treatment became more elaborate, doubtless because it was realized that

63

the light of moving candle-flames in association with cut crystal would produce a scintillating brilliance. The faceting was accordingly extended to sockets, pans and branches, and the effect was heightened by the addition of star-cutting.

In the second half of the century, styles remained comparatively simple until about 1770 but with a growing tendency to increase the quantity of cut pendant drops. But thereafter, these were considerably augmented, and cut pinnacles like lance-heads, usually three-sided, appeared in addition. At the same time, the protuberances on the shaft increased in length and decreased in diameter.

By this time, the other applied arts were displaying an enthusiastic dedication to the neo-classical style inaugurated chiefly by Robert Adam (q.v.), and it was not long before chandeliers embodied forms deriving from classical urns in the shafts, numerous chains or cut drops arranged like swags (q.v.), which both looped between the branches and swept downward and outward from the very top, and even large, flat drops cut in a manner suggestive of paterae (q.v.).

All this additional ornament naturally tended to conceal the central shaft, but in the early 19th century, it practically disappeared from view altogether, so that the effect of a chandelier depended less on its basic structure than its external, apparent form. In many chandeliers of the period, this form was conditioned not only by outward-curving chains of cut drops which appeared almost as a solid mass, but also by hanging curtains of drops, which began just beneath the top. There were sometimes several of these, one below another, the drops being suspended from the edges of large metal rings.

Chequered diamonds: a cutting design of the early 19th century involving the making of two opposed incisions on a flat-topped diamond to form four smaller diamonds. *See* Cut glass.

Cider glasses: until about the middle of the 18th century, expensive cider of high quality was drunk from any type of glass considered suitable by the drinker, but thereafter, occurred some degree of specialization which was quite literally superficial. The glass employed most frequently – though not exclusively – was the long-stemmed flute (q.v.) with attenuated round-funnel bowl, of a type which had appeared in about 1740. An identical vessel was used for strong beer or ale (q.q.v.) and was one of the several varieties considered suitable for sparkling champagne (q.v.). But flutes dedicated specifically to cider were wheel-engraved with appropriate motifs such as apple trees, branches or blossom, cider-barrels, and a broad-winged insect which was probably intended for a codlin moth. Very occasionally, the engraved word 'Cyder' appeared.

Feet were sometimes folded, and stems might be of plain, air-twist or opaque-twist (q.q.v.) construction, with or without knops. One form of embellishment, bearing witness to passions long since forgotten, was designed as propaganda against a proposed tax on cider, which came into force, notwithstanding, in 1763. This seems to have been initiated by the cider-manufacturers, and took the form of the engraved legend 'No Excise' in addition to other elements relating to the beverage. The tax was reduced three years later, but was not abolished altogether until the beginning of the reign of Queen Victoria.

Ordinary cider was usually drunk from tankards or mugs of various materials, but the superior variety served in glasses was very expensive and enjoyed something of the status of a wine.

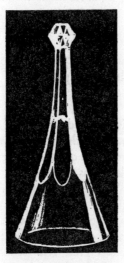

Coaching glass, c. 1800

Coaching glasses: in the late 18th century, stage-coaches began to be run with greatly increased efficiency owing to the competition of the

Mails, which, being immune from the payment of tolls, were virtually state-subsidized. The changing of horses was brought to a fine art and was normally achieved in three minutes or less, so that, with halts of such short duration, it was impossible for the passengers to visit the bar of the inn. Accordingly, if the landlord wished to do any business, he was obliged to send refreshment out to the coach.

The type of drinking glass used in this connection was identical with the contemporary glass stirrup-cup (q.v.), which differed from ordinary glasses in having no foot, the stem terminating in a small knop. Coaching glasses were brought out on a tray upside-down. They were handed to passengers, filled, emptied, and handed back again. The peculiar design was doubtless chosen through memories of heavy casualties among the normal glasses used previously, for there was nowhere inside or outside a coach where they could be set down with safety.

The earliest were usually cut with vertical fluting (q.v.) which ran from the knop to part of the way up the bowl, which was frequently conical. The knop itself was commonly faceted. This type continued to some extent into the 19th century, but it was not long before coaching glasses began to be cut with Regency motifs such as relief diamonds (q.v.). Many looked like small rummers with a ball knop instead of a foot.

Coin glasses: glasses enclosing a coin in a hollow part of the stem; from the late 17th century to the present day.

Coloured glass: glass is coloured by melting various metallic oxides with the other ingredients, and the technique was known in Egypt in the 15th century B.C., the results often showing a remarkable degree of sophistication. Such glass was produced later under the Roman Empire and in medieval Venice, but was never of any great quantitative importance in Britain.

In the late 17th century, George Ravenscroft (q.v.) and others made some coloured glass objects, one survivor of the period being a small decanter of purplish metal preserved in the Victoria and Albert Museum, London. Ravenscroft, of course, was still under the influence of the Venetian tradition. But even before he inaugurated his glass-of-lead, the selling end of the industry had been in the hands of men who understood their market very well, so the fact that so little coloured glass has survived compared with ordinary flint glass, can only mean that there was no great commercial demand for it. Indeed, the frequency with which glass was associated terminologically with crystal indicates quite clearly that its most esteemed characteristic was colourless transparency. The largest single group of glass artefacts was drinking glasses, and there seems little doubt that most British drinkers had no wish to destroy their visual enjoyment of good liquor by disguising its natural colour.

Some writers have endeavoured to prove that coloured glass vessels were common in the mid-18th century by quoting out of context some observations by Dr Richard Pococke in 1751 concerning glass-making at Stourbridge in Worcestershire, which included a reference to glass 'of all the capital colours'. A more extensive quotation, however, puts the matter in its right perspective: 'Stourbridge, famous for its glass manufactures, especially for its coloured glass, with which they make painted windows which is here coloured in the liquid, of all the capital colours in their several shades. . . .' Since Dr Pococke was speaking of window-glass, his observations can have no relevance to wine glasses, decanters, and other things. Stourbridge *may* have produced coloured drinking glasses, but Pococke's comments are useless as evidence of the fact.

Nevertheless, a few such items were fashioned from green metal from quite early in the 18th century, many of them being exported to the European mainland where they were more acceptable to popular taste than in Britain. Even 'Bristol blue' represented a mere drop in the ocean of national production, and one has to wait until the Victorian period for anything approaching an extensive manufacture of coloured glass vessels. *See* Oppenheim, Mayer.

Colour-twists: spirals of coloured enamel in the stems of appropriate objects, chiefly drinking glasses, from about 1765 to 1780, usually combined with twists of white enamel. *See* Opaque-twists.

Comb-fluting: narrow, closely-spaced vertical flutes encircling the base of a decanter, jug, etc., formed by cutting with a round-edged wheel. As the cutter reduced the pressure against the wheel at the end of each incision, it finished in a blunt point, giving the resultant pattern some resemblance to the teeth of a comb. Comb-fluting began to become popular in the 1760s, and represented a development from short, wide flutes which often embellished the lower parts of shouldered decanters (q.v.) a little after the middle of the 18th century. *See* Moulded fluting.

Comb-fluting

Comfit glasses: an early name for sweetmeat glasses (q.v.).

Comport: a variant of 'compote'; a term of no great antiquity in English glass terminology indicating a kind of vase-like object, usually with a cover, mounted on a stand, and used for serving nuts, sweetmeats and so forth. These vessels appeared at the end of the 18th century, before the term under discussion came into use, but were far more frequent from about 1815, when they tended to be lavishly decorated with relief diamonds and other cut patterns. *See* Cut glass.

Constables: an 18th-century colloquialism for drinking glasses of unusually large size, used either as loving cups on ceremonial occasions or for serving strong, spirituous liquor into smaller vessels such as firing glasses (q.v.).

Constables were immensely enlarged versions of stemmed glasses of all kinds, and an example mentioned by Hartshorne in *Old English Glasses* (1897), from Levens Hall, Westmorland, is in the form of a tall, plain-stemmed goblet with funnel-shaped bowl, the whole being no less than 38 cm high. This imposing vessel, which dates from about 1760, is engraved with the inscription *Levens High Constable*. The term occurs in an 18th-century round relating to a group of bibulous fellows toasting their mistresses. One of them considers that the capacity of an ordinary glass would do insufficient honour to his 'Phyllis', and the lyric ends with the lines: 'For a larger I'll soon change my cup; To the brim fill the Constable up.' In the last quarter of the 18th century when rummers (q.v.) began to attain great popularity, the proportions of constables changed, with the stems becoming short and the large bowls dominating the design. These glasses are usually known as serving-rummers.

Cordial glasses: from the late 17th century, it became the custom for large households to make their own cordials, which were an early equivalent of modern liqueurs. They consisted of various fruits, spices and herbs macerated in alcohol, which was usually brandy distilled from lees or from wine which had turned sour. Until the practice began to become widely established in the first quarter of the 18th century, ordinary dram glasses were used. These were glasses of small capacity used otherwise for common neat spirits such as gin, brandy and rum;

Cordial glass, c. 1710

Cordial glass, c. 1760

but in the second quarter of the century, the habit of consuming cordials after taking tea attained such popularity that large numbers of special cordial glasses were made to contain them. It was considered that the excessive consumption of tea occasioned 'dejection of spirits and flatulency', so that there was some show of medical sanction for taking a cheering and palatable antidote for these distressing symptoms. The antidote was resorted to with enthusiasm, especially by ladies.

Nearly all surviving 18th-century cordial glasses, apart from the earliest, are tall in the stem and with very small bowls (q.v.) of various kinds including flutes. The stems, which were generally without knops after about 1730, went through all the contemporary stages of development such as plain, air-twist, opaque-twist and cut. The drinking of cordials continued all over Britain into the 19th century, but later examples of cordial glasses were often indistinguishable from those used for ordinary spirits, and often took the form of miniature rummers. *See* Ratafia.

Cork: it is known that there was some kind of glass-making activity in Cork in 1761, but no artefacts have been identified and it seems probable that the venture was short-lived. It may, however, have had the beneficial effect of encouraging another attempt to found an industry when circumstances became more favourable, and this time arrived in 1780 when Ireland, which was not subject to the tax imposed by the Glass Excise Act of 1745 and doubled in 1770, was permitted to export any glass it might produce. These new circumstances enabled Irish glasshouses to compete with those of Britain on highly advantageous terms.

In 1782, Hayes Burnett and Rowe announced that they would commence manufacture in Cork the following year, and that all the necessary workmen and equipment were being brought over from England. The name of the firm was the Cork Glass Company, and certain of its more ordinary productions, such as mould-blown decanters, were marked underneath with the legend 'Cork Glass Company' or 'Cork Glass Co.', the words, imparted by reversed hollow lettering in the base of the mould, being arranged in a circle. It is probable, however, that this system of marking was not adopted immediately the company commenced operations in 1783. By no means all decanters were marked, either because they were free-blown instead of being blown into a mould, or because a plain mould was used instead of a lettered one.

Other objects cannot be distinguished with any certainty from their counterparts made elsewhere in Ireland and Britain, but certain characteristics typical of Cork provide some assistance. The most important of these is the vesica pattern, consisting of linked horizontal ovals pointed at the ends, and either joined immediately to each other or with a small lozenge or diamond-shape in between. The vesica was an ancient motif, used in Christian iconography in a vertical form to surround the heads of sacred personages, and occurring with remarkable frequency on Dutch brass alms dishes of the 17th century. But those who applied cut or engraved decoration to Cork decanters and jugs in the late 18th and early 19th centuries displayed a peculiar devotion to it.

Cork decanter, c. 1800

Another somewhat diagnostic feature was two or three double neck-rings on decanters. Other neck-rings are less useful as evidence, and consisted of triple rings, used also in Waterford and in Britain, round rings, used all over Europe as well as Britain, and square rings, which were common in Bristol.

The Cork Glass Company ceased operations in 1818, but meanwhile, another manufactory had opened in 1815. This was the Waterloo Glass Company, marked decanters bearing the words 'Waterloo Company Cork' or 'Waterloo Co. Cork'. These decanters were all of Prussian shape (*See* Decanters), and mostly had three triple neck-rings precisely like those of Waterford, and sometimes mushroom stoppers with ball knops which were used in Waterford as well as Britain. Here again, however, the vesica pattern is often of assistance in assigning an unmarked specimen to the Waterloo company, which closed down in 1836, almost certainly as a result of the extension of the Glass Excise Act to Ireland in 1825, which deprived the Irish glasshouses of their previous competitive advantages. Most mould-blown Irish decanters and jugs, including those made in Cork, had softened vertical flutes round their bases imparted by ribs on the inside of the moulds.

Cotton-twists: *See* Opaque-twists.

Crizzling or crisseling: a defect in glass which plagued Ravenscroft (q.v.) during the experimental phase of English lead crystal, due to an excess of alkaline flux in the composition of the metal. In bad cases the disease is progressive, and the glass eventually develops a white, foggy opacity. This defect is sometimes present even in glass of the 19th century.

Cross-cut diamonds: a cutting design of the early 19th century, rare because of the difficulty involved in its execution, consisting of relief diamonds (q.v.) with minute incisions of V-section bisecting the top angles. *See* Cut glass.

Crown glass: glass crowns often formed the basis for window-panes; they were of Levantine origin and began to be made in Northern Europe in the 14th century. They were formed by blowing a paraison or glass balloon, opening it transversely, and spinning it until it flattened and spread under the influence of centrifugal force. When detached from the blowing-iron, a rough knob remained in the centre. Rectangular or diamond-shaped panes were sometimes cut from the crown avoiding the knob, and the presence of lines of part-circular form are often to be seen on the panes of 18th-century bookcases, indicating a crown origin. Glaziers of windows were less particular, and the centre of the crown is frequently to be seen in the window-panes of old houses, though some represent later replacements.

Cruets: glass 'creuits', with and without feet, were among items ordered from Venice by the Glass Sellers' Company of London between 1667 and 1673, but we can have no idea what they were like. It was probably in the last decade of the 17th century that they began to be accommodated in silver frames whose hall marks enable us to date the glass as well as the silver, but the earliest survivors were made shortly before 1710. The cruets themselves, in plain glass, were shaped like miniature decanters, with the sides of the bodies sloping slightly inward to the base. Cutting began to be employed in the 1730s, and included large relief diamonds with such a low degree of projection that the transparency of the glass was unimpaired. Shallow facets were cut on the necks and shoulders from the middle of the century when the same treatment was prevalent on the stems of drinking glasses, and little change occurred in form or decoration until the 1780s. Cruets then became tall and tapering like contemporary decanters (q.v.) and were

Cruet, c. 1785

sometimes supported on feet. Cut facets were generally abandoned and were replaced by vertical fluting (q.v.), sometimes crossed by encircling, horizontal lines, which gave an appearance of barrel-staves and hoops. These cruets had great elegance in keeping with the slightly feminine grace of the prevailing neo-classical style. In the early 19th century, they abandoned the perpendicularity of the previous period and began to be profusely cut in the rather bristling manner of the Regency, with a high incidence of sharp relief diamonds and prismatic cutting which reflected as well as refracted. *See* Cut glass.

Crystallo-ceramie: ceramic bas-relief plaques embedded in clear glass. Such objects appear to have been first made in Bohemia in the 18th century, but the results were usually unattractive owing to distortion which occurred during cooling. In 1819, Apsley Pellatt (q.v.) took out a patent for fourteen years covering his process of manufacture, and crystallo-ceramie took on a new lease of life.

Toilet-water bottle with crystallo-ceramie, c. 1820

His productions were infinitely superior to the Bohemian versions, not only because he overcame the defects arising from differing rates of contraction of the ceramic substance and its glass covering while cooling, but also because the lead glass employed displayed a crystalline clarity. Pellatt called his plaques sulphides, and they frequently consisted of portraits of celebrities including members of the Royal family. In these cases, his technical skill and devoted care were of some importance, for it is unlikely that an effigy of a Royal princess with a bulging cheek as though she had mumps would have been well received. His productions appeared in many sizes and as parts of many objects including decanter-stoppers, mugs, paper-weights, goblets, doorknobs, and even ear-rings, and were sometimes cut in broad facets which enhanced the appearance of the enclosed ceramic medallion.

Crystallo-ceramie fell out of fashion in about 1835, but reappeared on the repeal of the Glass Excise Act in 1845 when taxation no longer deterred manufacturers from making heavy objects. These later productions, however, lacked the quality of Pellatt's work and eventually brought about an unfavourable reaction.

Cullet: broken glass added to the other ingredients in the batch (q.v.).

Cushion knop

Cushion knop: a small protuberance on the stem of a glass in the form of a flattened sphere, occurring at the top or bottom or both, and similar in proportions to a cushion or torus at the base of a certain type of classical column. *See* Stems.

Cut glass: the decorative cutting of glass by means of lapidaries' wheels was practised under the Roman Empire, but the development of lead crystal in Britain from 1675 was destined eventually to open a new phase in the art. The new English metal not only had far greater refractive brilliance than Continental soda glass, but was also considerably softer, so that it was ideally suited to cutting on both counts. Nevertheless, it was to be some years before cutting was executed on a significant scale in Britain, possibly because of an absence of experienced craftsmen of native origin capable of doing the work. In 1709, an attempt was made to hold an auction of imported German cut glass in London, but the sale had to be abandoned in the face of a violent demonstration by the London glass sellers. This incident may, however, have marked the beginning of a demand, for John Akerman (q.v.) was marketing cut-glass dessert utensils by the early 1720s, and cut chandeliers were on sale before 1730. The men who decorated British glass in the new manner for Akerman were Germans resident in London, but it may be presumed that it was not long before native cutters acquired the necessary skill in order to satisfy the constantly increasing demand.

It was probably in the late 1730s that Thomas Betts (q.v.) established his King's Arms Glass Shop at Charing Cross in London, and it was from here that he issued his elaborately engraved trade card listing the 'curious cut glass' which he made and sold. The list included almost everything but drinking glasses. It is generally assumed that although they were often cut, they were not considered worth mentioning because they were taken as read; but we cannot be certain of this, particularly as none appears to have survived, and there can be little doubt that the majority of such glasses at the time had plain or air-twist stems.

Most surviving British cut drinking glasses were made from about 1745 onwards, and in the early years, cutting was confined to the stem, as this was the thickest part and accordingly less liable to fracture during the cutting operation than the bowl or foot. Glass was cut by pressing it against a revolving iron wheel with wet sand fed on to it from above, and this involved powerful vibrations which would certainly have shattered a glass which was not properly annealed (*See* Annealing), and any glass at all if great skill and care were not exercised.

Cutting designs used in association with heavier objects such as bowls (q.v.) and dessert utensils consisted first of edge-scalloping and pointed serrations, and then shallow surface cutting in the form of LOW RELIEF DIAMONDS. The first patterns to appear on stems were HOLLOW

Low relief diamonds

FACETS in the shape of LOZENGES (DIAMONDS), followed shortly after by HEXAGONS. Having once been introduced, these forms of treatment persisted for the remainder of the 18th century on a large variety of objects, with the diamond facets enjoying more popularity than the hexagonal variety. After about 1780, both tended to be cut more deeply.

SCALE CUTTING appeared in about 1760, but its incidence was never anything but low, probably because it was more troublesome to execute.

Diamond facets

Hexagonal facets

After the middle of the century, it became customary to extend the cutting upwards to span the junction with the bowl, unless, of course, the latter was of round-funnel (q.v.) shape which would have rendered the device impossible of execution. The pattern employed for this upward extension consisted of short, straight-sided facets and is known as BRIDGE-FLUTING. Shortly after it was introduced, some expensive

Scale cutting

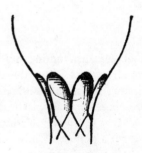

Bridge-fluting

glasses had the surfaces and sometimes the edges of their feet cut as well, and the growing experience and confidence of British cutters encouraged them, in some cases, to decorate the bowls with shallow facets which refracted light in a delightful fashion and enhanced the appearance of any light-coloured wine such as champagne.

From the late 1760s, even glasses with otherwise uncut bowls commonly had small oval or circular depressions known as PUNTS, cut all round just below the rim, usually with minute sprigs engraved between them.

At the same time, although cylindrical stems were the most numerous, some were embellished with a knop either in the centre or a short distance below the bowl, while the cut stems of candlesticks sometimes had a knop at the base. Elaborate goblets, which were often presentation-pieces, might have more than one of these protuberances in the stem, but were naturally uncommon. All these knops were cut, the flat planes usually meeting to form a horizontal ridge round the centre.

In about 1770, a new kind of stem-treatment was introduced in the form of six or occasionally seven cut vertical FLUTES running from

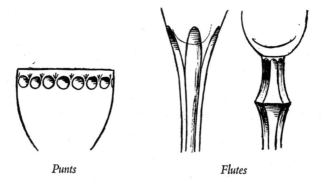

Punts   *Flutes*

bowl to foot and surmounting any knop that might be present. These flutes were always cut across the axis of the stem – a fact which is usually obvious on close examination. This cutting design was particularly pleasing, for although the diamond and hexagonal facets were too shallow to be obtrusive, the flutes followed the profile of the stem, bringing about a perfect alliance between form and decoration. They were mostly left plain, but might sometimes be horizontally sliced or notched across the dividing ridges. Flutes, which were named by analogy with the long, vertical hollows in the three original orders of classical columns, belonged to the classical revival, which gained general acceptance in the applied arts in about 1770.

Two other designs of classical origin which were introduced at the same time were known by glass-cutters as SPLITS and PRINTIES (q.q.v.). Splits were narrow incisions often cut vertically and arranged in a row round the bowls of glasses just below the rim as an integrated pattern. In this form, they sometimes occurred on Roman bowls, but they were used also in 18th-century Britain to form minor patterns ancillary to the main cutting design. Printies were circular or oval depressions, the punts already mentioned being miniature versions of the same thing. They appeared with great frequency in three rows round the shoulders of contemporary tapering decanters (q.v.) and the related type made in Belfast (q.v.), and more rarely on the bowls of rummers (q.v.) at the end of the 18th century.

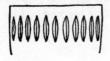

Splits and Printies

Meanwhile, the pre-existing facets, which were congruous with the earlier rococo style without representing a specific manifestation of it, endured on the stems of drinking glasses until the end of the 18th century and even to some extent into the Regency period.

In strict historical terms the Regency began in 1811 and ended in 1820, when the mentally-incapacitated George III died and was succeeded by the Regent as George IV. It is used, however, as a convenient label for a stylistic phase, which began in about 1800 and degenerated out of existence in the 1830s. It brought a different approach to the cut decoration of glass, and many new designs, the work being greatly facilitated by the general application of steam-power before 1810.

One of the first and most long-lived cutting designs of this new phase was a radically-modified rendering of a design which had already appeared in the first half of the 18th century – RELIEF DIAMONDS. The earlier versions were large, and rose to only a trifling extent above the surface, so that the reflection of light was minimized out of respect for crystalline transparency. The diamonds were now smaller, higher, and more acutely pointed. They were produced by cutting deep, narrow channels with mitre-wheels having edges shaped like the top of a triangle. These channels, which were in immediate contact with each other, were then crossed by others more or less at right-angles, resulting in a field of sharp pyramids, the extreme points of which represented the original surface of the glass. The immediate inspiration for this design may have come from reserves filled with tiny diamonds of similar construction but in low relief, which occurred on decanters (q.v.) made at Waterford and elsewhere in the late 18th century. These very small diamonds were sometimes found on drinking glasses of various kinds.

In about 1815, a modification was introduced resulting in what are called CROSS-CUT DIAMONDS. Opposed incisions were made with a very

 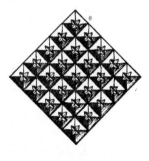

Relief diamonds   *Cross-cut diamonds*

small mitre-edged wheel across the very apex of each relief diamond so that they bisected the top angles. Not only was the process exceedingly difficult, but it was also attended by the risk of ruining an object when it was almost finished, so it is hardly surprising that cross-cut diamonds should have been somewhat rare and are seldom found on surviving artefacts of the period. This design had first appeared in embryo in the 18th century when the almost flat, earlier relief diamonds were sometimes cut across the top with little risk.

The next development consisted of the embellishment of a flat-topped diamond. This was formed by making the incisions with the mitre-wheel further apart, so that an uncut zone was left between them. Within the limits of the Georgian period, this lozenge-shaped zone was never left plain, and the first type of decoration to be applied to it produced a design known as STRAWBERRY DIAMONDS, which was made by cutting a field of smaller diamonds, usually sixteen in number, on the flat top. A less elaborate version called CHEQUERED DIAMONDS had four larger diamonds instead, and necessitated only two incisions, one at right-angles to the other. Strawberry diamonds occurred with great frequency in the early 19th century, but the same could not be said of the next design.

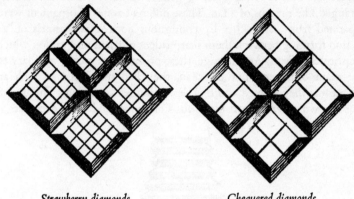

Strawberry diamonds   *Chequered diamonds*

This was the HOBNAIL PATTERN, a name which is widely misused. It existed in two main versions. The simpler was formed by cutting two V-section incisions which crossed the flat-topped diamond diagonally from corner to corner, while the other had two more incisions which

Hobnail pattern; both types

81

met the sides at right-angles and produced an eight-pointed star in intaglio. The hobnail pattern was not used before about 1820 and does not appear to have enjoyed any great popularity, judging by the paucity of surviving examples.

From the beginning of the 19th century, it had been customary for large objects such as decanters to bear more than one kind of cut decoration. The shoulders, for example, might be cut with broad flutes, the centre of the body with a field of relief diamonds, and the base with a circuit of COMB-FLUTING (q.v.) or groups of narrow incisions (SPLITS) arranged like the ribs of a fan. These different zones of ornament were separated from each other by contiguous horizontal channels of V-section forming between them sharp ridges of triangular section which constituted prisms. At this stage, these prisms were merely ancillary to the main ornament, but by 1820, they had multiplied to such an extent that they formed a cutting design in their own right. This design was known as PRISMATIC CUTTING. On the shoulders of decanters it

Prismatic cutting

looked somewhat like steps, a circumstance which has led some of the less well-informed members of the antiques trade to apply to it the incorrect jargon name 'step-cutting'. Prismatic cutting occurred on jugs and other vessels as well as decanters, but never formed complete circuits on jugs owing to the presence of the handle. It was not invariably horizontal, and was sometimes found in vertical form encircling the base of a decanter as an alternative to comb-fluting, and in unconnected groups on other objects.

Comb-fluting remained acceptable well into the 19th century, but shortly after 1800 a related pattern, differing from it only in degree, began to be used as a substitute. The pointed flutes, which were narrower and more numerous than in comb-fluting, were either vertical or slanting and often rose and fell in zigzag fashion. These were known as BLAZES.

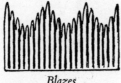

Blazes

REEDING or PILLAR MOULDING occurred in the early 19th century on objects of appropriate shape, but did not attract much interest until shortly before 1830. The pattern consisted of a circuit of pilasters of almost semicircular section. It was occasionally formed by cutting, but chiefly by blowing the paraison (q.v.) into a mould with flutes all round the inside, especially in the later versions. It was found with great frequency on jugs and cylindrical decanters from about 1825 onwards.

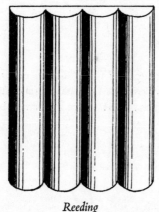

Reeding

In modern times, this design is often miscalled 'pillar fluting': a name which is almost a contradiction in terms, since pillars are convex and flutes are concave.

Cylinder knop: a thick, cylindrical protuberance, rounded at each end, sometimes forming the main stem-feature on glasses of the early 18th century. The originals of the species were of heavy construction,

Cylinder knop

their bulky appearance being often mitigated by the presence of a tear-shaped air bubble; but slighter versions, usually surmounted by bell-shaped bowls, began to be made in the second decade of the century. *See* Stems.

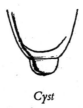

Cyst

Cyst: a formation created by manipulation occurring at the base of certain drinking-glass bowls in the early 18th century, and consisting of a narrower portion than that above it, formed by constriction.

D

Dagnia: a glass-making family from Mantua, but which probably came originally from the glass centre of Altare near Genoa, introduced into England by Sir Robert Mansell (q.v.) in about 1630. Three of them became established in Newcastle upon Tyne (q.v.) late in the reign of Charles II, and commenced operations in the Closegate glasshouse in 1684. It was from these beginnings that a very distinguished glass industry developed in the 18th century.

Decanters: to decant originally meant to transfer liquid to another vessel by 'canting', or tilting, the container; but it was not until the last decade of the 17th century that the name 'decanter' came to be applied to what had been regarded previously as a superior kind of bottle in which liquor was served at table.

Shaft-and-globe decanter, c. 1680

Ravenscroft (q.v.) mentioned 'bottles' of the kind under discussion in his list of 1677, as the more familiar name had, at that time, not yet come into use. But it is convenient to use the later term retrospectively to cover his productions, as they were made of lead crystal, usually colourless, and were of infinitely higher quality than ordinary bottles.

Even before the advent of lead glass, decanters made of soda metal had been of what is known as SHAFT-AND-GLOBE shape, with narrow, cylindrical necks and quasi-spherical bodies, and this shape remained the most popular well into the 18th century. Ravenscroft undertook to supply them with stoppers and either with or without handles. He and his 17th-century successors usually made them either with gadroon-like ribs rising vertically from the bottom to almost half-way up the body, or covered all over with a net-like raised pattern which he called 'nipt diamond waies'. A surviving specimen of the latter sort, made by Ravenscroft himself, is preserved in the British Museum. A narrow glass ring was applied round the top of the neck as in the case of ordinary bottles, but, unlike bottles, some were supported on a rim-foot.

The other type of contemporary decanter was in the form of a JUG with a cylindrical body expanding upward from the base, and rounded shoulders which curved inward to the short cylindrical neck. This was topped by a wide pouring-mouth pinched into a spout on the side opposite the handle. Surviving stoppers, which are understandably rare, consist of a hollow cone which goes well down inside the neck, surmounted by a large mushroom-like finial with gadrooned edges, crowned by a ball knop or diminishing rings. Both these kinds of decanters might be decorated with 'extraordinary work', which added to the cost, and comprised applied trails in the form of lines or chains, a raised trellis pattern, frilled collars, and raspberry prunts (q.v.).

Surface ornament of the sort described, which was under strong Venetian influence, ceased to exert any appeal in the early 18th century. The jug-like decanter fell out of production, but the plain shaft-and-globe endured until the middle of the century with a lower kick (q.v.) in the base and a greater slope in the shoulders.

The next type was the MALLET-SHAPED DECANTER. It is not quite certain when it was first introduced, but it was well established by 1730.

Jug decanter, c. 1680   *Mallet-shaped decanter, c. 1730*

The neck was like that of its predecessors, but the body had almost horizontal shoulders and straight sides which were either vertical, or sloping outward to the base on free-blown examples, giving such a decanter the appearance of a sculptor's or mason's mallet. Some were of circular section, while others were polygonal with faceted sides, which were formed by blowing the paraison (q.v.) into a mould of appropriate shape, like many bottles of the imperial Roman era. All were made of very thick glass and had a rough pontil mark (q.v.) underneath, in the centre of a kick which diminished in height with the passage of time. Like the shaft-and-globe decanters before them, these also were sometimes equipped with a handle, and when this was present, a spout was often formed on the opposite side of the neck. The type of stopper accompanying mallet-shaped decanters must remain largely a matter of conjecture, though it is possible that it had a solid ball finial, sometimes containing small air bubbles. Some may not have had stoppers at all.

Cruciform decanter, c. 1750

CRUCIFORM decanters were a sub-species of the mallet shape, and were in production from about 1740 to 1760. The body of this type was shaped in section like a Greek cross, instead of being circular or polygonal. This formation was not a matter of stylistic caprice, but had the functional purpose of exposing a larger area of glass to the iced water in the wine-cistern. Cruciform decanters were evidently mould-blown, and a variety which developed from them was formed in the same way. This related type had four broad sides with a deep vertical channel each side of the canted corners. On these later representatives of the mallet-shaped species, which were taller in relation to their width, the neck often bore a wide ring near the top tooled into a multiple formation so that it looked like several rings in close contact.

After 1750, all decanters of good quality, whatever their shape, were 'hollowed', that is to say, the pontil scar was ground off the base which was then smoothly polished.

Chinese porcelain bottles probably provided the inspiration for what were advertised as SHOULDERED DECANTERS, which first appeared in

Shouldered decanter, c. 1750

about 1745. They differed from the mallet shape in having shoulders with a pronounced downward slope, while the top of the neck was usually without any sort of applied glass ring. In rare instances, the body had vertical sides, but it generally sloped outward or inward to the base, the shoulders, in the former variety, being slightly narrower in order to adjust the capacity. These shouldered decanters with outward sloping sides are often miscalled 'mallet-shaped' in auctioneers' catalogues.

The earliest stoppers were in the form of short spires, easily distinguishable from the larger spire-stoppers of the 19th century, or narrow cylinders with flat tops. Many of these decanters were plain of surface, but cut decoration soon began to be applied to them in keeping with contemporary drinking glasses. Short, wide flutes might encircle the base (*See* Fluting), the neck and shoulders might be faceted, while the main part of the body might bear circuits of incisions grouped to form stars or sunbursts. The central zone was sometimes decorated with engraving, which included such motifs as fruiting vines, instead of cut ornament, and from the middle of the 18th century this engraving frequently took the form of imitation bottle tickets in a more florid rendering of the silver originals. Silver bottle tickets, engraved or pierced with the name of the contents such as Ale, Punch, Port and so forth, were hung round the necks of decanters by thin silver chains, and representations of these chains were commonly engraved in conventionalized form ostensibly supporting the engraved escutcheon bearing the name of the liquor for which the decanter was intended. Later, these bottle tickets were sometimes executed in white or coloured enamel (*See* Beilby). Decanters embellished in this manner by engraving or enamelling were known as Label decanters.

All-over facet-cutting began to be applied from about 1750, usually in the form of shallow diamonds, hexagonal facets being chiefly confined to the necks of decanters which were not cut all over. Shallow cutting also decorated the spire stopper, but shortly after 1760, this type went out of fashion, and was replaced by a flat, vertical disc, which might be left plain at first but was soon given slight cutting on the flat sides and faceting or slicing round the edge. Another shape for stopper-finials appeared soon after, continuing as an alternative to the vertical disc, and was somewhat like a kite or a Norman shield. These are sometimes described as 'pear-shaped', but in view of their flatness, this description is scarcely apt. Other flat finials might be in the form of lozenges, trefoils, or hearts.

The diamond facets on decanters which were cut all over commonly ceased just above the inward curve of the shoulders, giving way to a circuit of short flutes which were easier to cut on a slightly concave surface. Above these, the facets recommenced and continued almost to the top of the neck. Diamond facets were almost invariably longer one way than the other. They ran horizontally on the body and vertically on the neck.

An oddity among shouldered decanters was the ICE DECANTER, which was primarily intended for the service of champagne, though it would have been suitable for any other wine which benefited from cooling. It was first advertised in 1755, but does not seem to have enjoyed any widespread popularity despite its ingenious, if unattractive built-in cooling device. This consisted of a bladder-shaped glass container situated inside the body of the decanter and looking distressingly like a pathological cyst. It was filled with pieces of ice through a circular aperture in the shoulder of the decanter, and was closed by a wide cork with a metal cap having a small ring-handle. When the decanter was filled with wine, the liquor surrounded the ice-container which cooled it very efficiently. The advantage of this device was that the decanter did not have to be lifted dripping from the iced water in a wine-cistern; but it is unlikely that ice decanters were made much after 1770, and survivors are so seldom encountered that one can only assume that their production was on a limited scale.

At about the same time as the above developments occurred, the TAPERING (TAPER, TAPERED) DECANTER appeared, and became the most

Ice decanter, c. 1760   *Tapering decanter, c. 1780*

popular type of the neo-classical phase associated with the name of Robert Adam (q.v.). The shoulders practically disappeared altogether, so that the neck merged into the body without interruption. Entirely plain examples were made, but comb-fluting (q.v.) often encircled the base of the body, while the neck might be covered with diamond or hexagonal facets; but by the beginning of the last quarter of the 18th century, this part was more usually fluted (*See* Fluting). Neo-classical motifs seldom appeared on decanters in the form of cutting, but some were engraved round the body with looping swags, paterae (q.q.v.), and other typical elements of the style, though ornament of this kind was rare. Some of these decanters had several circuits of printies running round the top of the shoulders. Accompanying stoppers, which might be vertical discs or kite-shaped, mostly had bevelled edges.

In 1775, a London glass seller named Christopher Haedy, who was probably the son of an immigrant German cutter who had worked for Akerman (q.v.) earlier in the century, put an advertisement in the *Bath Chronicle* which mentioned, among other items, 'vases with square feet' and 'curious barrel-shaped decanters cut on an entire new pattern'. At the period in question, 'curious' was practically a synonym for 'new-fashioned', so it can be assumed, not that Haedy had invented barrel-shaped decanters, but that they had not been in existence for very long at the time of his advertisement.

The form of BARREL-SHAPED DECANTERS derived from that of the contemporary wine-barrel, which was long and narrow, and a few such decanters have survived cut from top to bottom with vertical flutes, crossed at regular intervals by encircling channels. This must have been the 'entire new pattern' and it occurred at the same time on cruets (q.v.) and other objects of suitable shape. On Haedy's decanters, it heightened the affinity with barrels by suggesting staves and hoops. Already, in about 1770, certain facet-cut shouldered decanters of attenuated form had begun to approach the barrel shape, but there is no doubt that Haedy's cut fluting was more in keeping with the clean elegance of the neo-classical style.

Despite their attractive appearance, comparatively few barrel-shaped decanters have survived, partly, perhaps, on account of a high casualty-rate resulting from a certain lack of stability.

Haedy's reference, in the same advertisement, to 'vases with square feet', reminds us that a few tall decanters of the period derived their form from that of classical urns or vases, and were sometimes supported on short stems and square feet like many original classical objects found during the excavations of Herculaneum and Pompeii. These decanters were probably the least common of all and are now exceedingly rare. They must have been very expensive and lacked stability, and it is also possible that contemporary taste considered that they looked more like objects of art than functional containers for wine.

SHIPS' DECANTERS began to be made some time in the second half of the 18th century, but nothing is heard of them before the Battle of Cape St Vincent in 1780, so it is probable that they had not been in

Barrel-shaped decanter, c. 1780   *Ship's decanter, c. 1790*

existence very long before this. Thereafter, they were often called RODNEY DECANTERS or simply Rodneys, as a compliment to the celebrated Admiral who won the battle. Elegant glassware was considered as desirable on board ship as on land, but ordinary decanters had little chance of remaining upright on a cabin-table. Ships' decanters were accordingly produced with wide bases up to 30 cm in diameter, with sides sloping inward to the bottom of the neck at an angle of about forty-five degrees. As with orthodox decanters, the earliest were often without neck-rings, but the latter soon became a standard feature, while cut decoration and stopper-design evolved in the normal way. Ships' decanters continued in demand into the mid-Victorian period, and a great many unconvincing reproductions have been manufactured in recent years.

An advertisement of 1784 mentioned 'barrel and Prussian-shaped decanters'. It is necessary to make the point because several writers on old glass have confused the two and treated them as being identical, whereas the wording of the advertisement makes it clear that a distinction was drawn between them. The PRUSSIAN-SHAPED DECANTER,

Prussian-shaped decanter, c. 1810

which appeared in England in about 1780 and was the first type to be made by the English staff of the Waterford (q.v.) glasshouse from 1783, had a body which was shaped, not like an 18th-century wine barrel, but like a squat cask. Neck-rings (q.v.), which were designed to provide a firm grip and which had already appeared on certain late shouldered decanters, now became an established feature. The majority were half-round in section, but others might be triangular, square, single, triple, or double, and were usually two or three in number.

Although vertical disc or kite-shaped stoppers continued with various modifications into the 19th century, an alternative, shaped like a mushroom, began to achieve popularity in the last decade of the 18th century. The cap of the 'mushroom' was never left plain, and was usually cut or moulded with radial incisions, and other designs after

1800. The shank of such a stopper sometimes had a small ball knop, and this type was especially favoured in Waterford, though it occurred in many other places at the same time.

Prussian-shaped decanters were made in large numbers from the time of their introduction until after 1830, their period of origin being generally deducible from the style and quantity of cut decoration (*See* Cut glass), among which, relief diamonds were immensely prevalent.

Meanwhile, a CYLINDRICAL DECANTER had come into production at the end of the 18th century, but although the shape of the body necessitated an angular change of direction at the shoulders, it was cut

Cylindrical decanter, c. 1815

in much the same way as the Prussian shape, but with a higher incidence of reeding (q.v.) and fluting, which were more easily carried out on an object with straight sides.

From the beginning of the 19th century, certain cylindrical decanters, chiefly of pint-size, were made with very short necks. Even on these, neck-rings often occurred, but they had little functional purpose, as the wide pouring-lip, which had been common since about 1780, effectively prevented the decanter from slipping out of the user's grasp. In the 1820s, these small decanters were sometimes recessed near the base to form an ostensible foot. With noticeable frequency, the sides of these and other late examples of the same species were covered with heavy reeding. After 1800, even some decanters of normal quart-size were occasionally furnished with rudimentary necks, especially in Bristol, but the bodies tended to be somewhat barrel-shaped rather than cylindrical.

In 1829, Apsley Pellatt (q.v.) issued a list of 'Net Cash Prices for the best Flint Glass Ware', and this included three decanters presumably of fairly recent design. One was called the NELSON SHAPE. It was of cylin-

Nelson shape, c. 1830

drical form widening slightly from the base to the angular shoulders, and cut all over with bold, vertical flutes. A large single ring was positioned at the base of the neck, and the stopper, which was also fluted, expanded outward to the widest part of the finial in a hollow curve, so that it had the shape of a wide-mouthed trumpet, the top being in the form of a compressed dome. This type of stopper, which was introduced in about 1820, was known at the time as 'turned out'.

The ROYAL SHAPE, which figured in the same advertisement, was of the same basic form but had three neck-rings which might be cut or plain, and slight cutting might also occur on the neck between them. Variations of these two types were manufactured in very large numbers, their production extending into the Victorian period, when the accompanying stoppers might have heavy ball-finials, bulbous versions of the mushroom, or large spires, either cut or plain.

A spire-shaped stopper was shown with another decanter in Pellatt's advertisement called the FANCY SHAPE. The body had a profile similar to that of the Prussian shape, but it had only one large and rather useless ring at the base of the neck, which had concave sides like a spool. It was cut with very wide flutes extending from base to pouring-lip and the heavy spire stopper was treated in the same way.

Fancy shape, c. 1830

Hybrids between the Nelson, Royal and Fancy shapes and pre-existing designs occurred on a considerable scale, together with later elements, some of which displayed unmistakable degeneracy, especially in the early Victorian period.

Makers of pressed glass, a process introduced from the United States in the 1830s, often made unconvincing attempts at reproducing late Georgian forms and cutting, and a general stylistic uncertainty prevailed in the design of decanters until the middle of the 19th century, when the wheel turned full circle. The shaft-and-globe shape, which we first encountered in the reign of Charles II, was then revived, mostly with very pleasing results, and retained its popularity up to the end of the century.

Deceptive glasses: drinking vessels which hold less than their outward dimensions suggest owing to the deliberate thickening of the glass. Rare examples have survived from the late 17th century. *See* Sham drams and Toastmasters' glasses.

Decolourising: all glass has a certain degree of natural colour arising from the presence of impurities, even after great care has been taken to ensure that the raw materials contain as little of these as possible. The chief enemy of the water-like brilliance sought after in crystal glass has always been iron oxide, and much early British glass was greenish in tint as a result of its presence. Decolourising was not widely practised in Britain until the early 18th century, although the technique itself was of some antiquity. It consisted of adding manganese dioxide to the usual constituents, so that the yellow and blue light, transmitted by the iron and which by optical mixing formed green, were apparently neutralized by the redder light from the other end of the spectrum. The process was applied to most glass of good quality, but throughout the 18th century and even in the early 19th century was sometimes deemed superfluous, with a resultant murkiness of tint.

Dishes: glass dishes and plates were known in Britain in the 16th century. Verzelini (q.v.) made some, and in 1588, the Earl of Leicester possessed eight with engraved rims, none of which has survived. After the establishment of a truly English glass industry in the late 17th century, they were regular items of production, but survivals in any number do not begin before the Regency. Before the advent of pressed glass in the 1830s, dishes were blown into shallow metal moulds. Apsley Pellatt (q.v.) advertised several types of more or less oval or oblong shape, the first having scalloped edges, the second gadrooned. Pellatt described the latter as 'pillar moulded'. Glass dishes are usually lacking in artistic interest and seldom attract the attention of collectors.

Domed foot: feet in the form of a dome began to occur on candlesticks, drinking glasses, sweetmeat glasses and other objects from the beginning of the 18th century, usually, in the first decade or so, with a fold or welt round the edge. With drinking glasses, the fashion did not generally endure much after 1720.

Donovan, James: an Irish enamel-painter of the late 18th century who owned a glasshouse near Dublin and is known to have decorated ceramics. He was probably the author of some contemporary enamelled glass, but there is insufficient evidence for specific attributions.

Dossie, Robert: author of *Handmaid to the Arts* (1758 and 1764) which contains, in particular, many observations concerning the contemporary British glass industry.

Double knop

Double knop: a stem-formation of the late 17th century comprising two ball knops or compressed ball knops in close proximity. A modified version occurred with some frequency on air-twist (q.v.) stems in the 18th century. *See* Stems.

Double ogee bowl: the bowl of a sweetmeat glass, drinking glass etc., with the sides flexed into a double curve from the narrow base to the wide brim. *See* Bowls of glasses.

Double-series twist: a formation in an air-twist or opaque-twist (q.q.v.) stem consisting of a central column with other twists spiralling round it.

Dram glasses: small glasses for 'dramming', or drinking spirits. They existed in various forms before the introduction of lead crystal, but tended, from the late 17th century onwards, to be miniature versions of wine glasses, though some took the form of diminutive tumblers in the late 18th century. *See* Cordial glasses.

Drawn stems: known otherwise in the 18th century as Straw shanks, describing a stem which was drawn from the thick mass of glass at the base of, for example, the bowl of a drinking glass. Drawn stems, chiefly of simple cylindrical form, became numerous in the first quarter of the 18th century, and were usual on later cut glasses. *See* Stuck shanks.

Drinking glasses: these are illustrated under Stems and discussed under specific headings such as Flute glasses, Dram glasses, Rummers, etc.

Drop knop

Drop knop: a protuberance on the stems of the late 17th and early 18th centuries in the form of a truncated cone, sometimes containing an air-bubble. The drop knop in Britain may have been inspired by a similar formation occasionally found on Dutch roemers (q.v.) in the 17th century. *See* Stems.

Drunrea: *See* Belfast.

Dublin: it is known that glass was made in Dublin in the 17th century, for, in 1691, Philip Roche assumed control of an existing glasshouse; but none of its productions has ever been identified and it is doubtful if they displayed any special characteristics. The most important venture of all was that of Charles Mulvaney, who commenced operations in 1785. Some of his manufactures, such as mould-blown decanters, were marked underneath 'C M Co.', but unmarked objects cannot be distinguished from those made elsewhere.

The same can be said of J. D. Ayckbower, who opened a glasshouse in 1799. Apart from some specimens marked 'Ayckbower Dublin' or 'J. D. Ayckbower Dublin', his productions cannot be identified. Dublin glasshouses never achieved the same success as those of Cork and Waterford (q.q.v.).

Dyer's Cross: a hamlet near Chiddingfold in Surrey where a Norman glassmaker, Laurence Vitrearius (q.v.), settled in about 1226 and founded an organized Wealden glass industry. In about 1240 he obtained an order for the supply of window-glass for the Abbey of St Peter, Westminster.

E

Edkins, Michael (1734–1811): glass-enameller. In Bristol, in the second half of the 18th century, there were a number of anonymous practitioners of the art of decorating glass with vitreous enamel, but Michael Edkins, whose career is fairly well documented, appears to have been pre-eminent. It seems likely that he was born in Birmingham in about 1734, and moved to Bristol shortly before 1755. In that year he married Betty James, the daughter of a local glass-maker: a successful union from several standpoints, in that it was the cause of his being granted citizenship in 1756, and resulted, over ensuing years, in the birth of thirty-three children.

He began his artistic career in Bristol as a decorator of delftware plates and ornaments and of Flemish tiles, for a potter named Richard Frank; but it is evident that he must have started his own business by 1761, for in that year he engaged an apprentice. Entries in his ledgers, which date from 1762, show that after beginning by decorating a post chaise with gilt ornaments, crests and monograms for a local potter, he soon became busy with his proper *métier* of enamelling blue and opaque white glass for several commercial undertakings, and one of them, the Redcliffe Backs glasshouse, employed his talents consistently from 1762 to 1787.

The objects to which his decoration was applied consisted of such items as beakers, cans, basins, jugs, bulb-glasses, jars and tea-caddies. Unfortunately, however, the study of Michael Edkins presents the frustrating problem that, although we know his life and career, at least in broad outline, we have no means of identifying his work with certainty, for unlike the Beilbys (q.v.) of Newcastle upon Tyne, he never used either a signature or a mark to indicate his authorship. On the other hand, several surviving specimens of tea-caddies, which remained for many years in the possession of his descendants, can be attributed to him with practical certainty, and these enable other examples to be identified by analogy with a minimum of doubt. Two are preserved in the Victoria and Albert Museum, London. These are in opaque white glass and are decorated with birds and flowers, the foliage of the latter showing a light-hearted curl at the end of almost every leaf, which was highly characteristic.

At a time when vases and other objects were frequently ornamented in the Chinese manner in imitation of porcelain, Michael Edkins must almost certainly, in the course of his career, have executed work in the same idiom. But as none can be identified beyond doubt, one is reduced to basing tentative attributions on the quality and style of the painting, a process which may, on occasion, do scant justice to other artists of the same period.

It is sometimes contended that as many of the objects decorated by Edkins make some show of masquerading as porcelain, they demonstrate, *ipso facto*, a lack of artistic integrity; but it could be contended with equal validity that since they do not set out to deceive anybody and are undoubtedly objects of both craftsmanship and art, they may be said to stand on their own merits as worthy artefacts. *See* Opaque glass.

Edwards, Benjamin: *See* Belfast.

Enamelled glass: the decorative enamelling of glass must be distinguished from painting, which eventually becomes worn off the surface to which it is applied. The enamel employed consisted of various metallic oxides melted with glass and ground into a powder to form a frit. This was then mixed with a flux and a liquid medium and applied to the object concerned like paint. When fired in a kiln, the enamel, which melted at a lower temperature than the glass, was fused into the surface and vitrified, becoming an integral part of the object. The technique was practised to some extent under the Roman Empire and with great skill by later Islamic artists. From the Eastern Mediterranean, it passed to Venice some time in the 15th century, and after 1500, spread to the Habsburg Empire where it attained great popularity in the 17th century. It reached Britain from Germany about the middle of the 18th century. *See* Beilby, Edkins, and Opaque glass.

Enamel-twists: *See* Opaque-twists.

Engraving, diamond: the drawing of designs on glass by scratching the surface with a diamond was probably first practised in Britain in the last quarter of the 16th century. Certain drinking glasses by Verzelini (q.v.) were treated in this manner, probably by an immigrant Frenchman named Anthony de Lysle. The earliest is dated 1577. Later examples of any period are scarce; first, because there were few native exponents of the art; secondly, because wheel-engraving was preferred in the 18th century. The engraved decoration on the Royal Oak goblet and the Exeter and Scudamore flutes of the reign of Charles II may have been the work of Dutch artists resident in England.

Among British glasses bearing emblems and inscriptions relative to the Jacobite cause, a small group known as 'Amen glasses' were diamond-engraved in about 1745. By this time, wheel-engraving was well established, and the alternative technique was probably employed, not because the artistic effect was preferred, but because it was more convenient for the large amount of lettering involved in rendering the verses of the Jacobite hymn. *See* Jacobite glass.

Engraving, stipple: it is unlikely that stipple engraving on glass was ever done by British craftsmen in the Georgian period, and the technique is mentioned here only because some Newcastle glasses were decorated in this manner in Holland in the 18th century. A full effect of chiaroscuro was achieved by making minute chips in the surface with a diamond or pointed steel tool, the chips being massed together for the highlights and lessening in concentration down to the shadows, which were made by the untouched surface of the glass. This engraving has great delicacy and gives the impression of having been blown on to the glass. *See* Greenwood.

Engraving, wheel: wheel-engraving is similar in principle to glass-cutting, in that both are executed by pressing the glass object against a revolving wheel fed with abrasive. Engraving wheels, however, are of small size and usually made of copper. A certain amount of wheel-engraving was carried out in Britain in the last decade of the 17th century, and consisted chiefly of inscriptions and occasional heraldry, but it achieved no sort of popularity until the second quarter of the 18th century. Designs then tended to become more ambitious, but British engraving on glass never reached the same standard as similar work executed in the Netherlands. The engraved surface was normally left matt so that the design contrasted in texture with the surrounding smooth glass, but in certain Jacobite motifs such as the rose, some parts were often polished. *See* Jacobite glass.

Ensall or Ensell, George: the 18th-century descendant of an immigrant glass-worker from Lorraine who was brought to England in the 16th century by Jean Carré (q.v.). *See* Annealing.

Epergnes: *See* Centrepieces.

Excise: *See* Glass Excise Act.

F

Façon de Venise: a name given to glass in a generally somewhat muted version of the Venetian style, made in various parts of Europe in the 16th and 17th centuries. It is sometimes difficult to distinguish from true Venetian work.

Feet: the feet of stemmed glass objects such as sweetmeat glasses, salvers and candlesticks (q.q.v.) had a general similarity to those of drinking glasses and were mostly circular and conical, with some variation in height. From the late 17th century to about the middle of the 18th century, a fold or welt usually occurred all round the circumference with a small air-space at the turn-over. This added greatly to the strength of the foot as it imparted a shock-absorbent quality to the edge, which was accordingly practically immune from chipping. When a chip appears to be present on the edge of such a foot it is almost invariably a small air-bubble which has fractured. The fold became uncommon after the Glass Excise Act (q.v.) of 1745, but never disappeared altogether.

At the beginning of the 18th century some feet were given a domed formation. This persisted on salvers, but scarcely endured beyond the 1720s on drinking glasses.

Firing glasses (q.v.) which appeared in about 1730, had plain, circular feet of unusual thickness, and a similar type occurred on ships' glasses (q.v.) and others to enhance their stability. A few glasses had oversewn, overstrung, or terraced (q.q.v.) feet, but these were uncommon.

In the last quarter of the 18th century, when the applied arts were subjected to the neo-classical influence introduced chiefly by Robert Adam (q.v.), the feet of numerous glass objects were square, often surmounted by a hollow dome, moulded underneath with radial flutes or channels of V-section. A modified version, of lozenge-shape, was found beneath elongated vessels such as salts and certain standing bowls. The square foot remained popular in the early 19th century, but feet of circular shape were always more numerous, though generally somewhat flatter than those of the 18th century.

Finger bowls or finger cups: it is uncertain when glass bowls for water in which the fingers were washed at meals were first introduced in the 18th century. There is a strong tradition that Jacobites were in the habit of pledging the absent claimant to the throne by passing their glasses over the finger bowls in symbolic allusion to 'the King over the water'; but no such bowls have survived from before the latter part of the century, or, if they have, cannot be positively associated with their purpose, since one small bowl in clear glass is much like another.

The late W. A. Thorpe believed that their identity may have been concealed under the name 'water glasses' in bills of the first half of the 18th century, but we cannot be certain of this. We can, however, be tolerably certain that they were of little artistic interest until they began to be made of blue and opaque glass with painted or gilt decoration in the second half of the century at Bristol and elsewhere. At the same time and in the early 19th century, finger bowls often bore cut decoration, but it is necessary to distinguish these more numerous survivors from individual wine-glass coolers (q.v.). The latter were of similar proportions but were provided with one or two pouring-lips, whereas finger bowls had none. *See* Jacobs, Isaac.

Firing glass, c. 1740

Firing glasses: these small glasses, which first appeared in about 1730 and were used not only for drinking, but also for banging on the table to express approbation of a speech, song, or toast, were mainly found in Masonic lodges and the clubs which abounded in London and other cities in the 18th and 19th centuries. When a number of people displayed their enthusiasm in this fashion, the sound was somewhat suggestive of a ragged volley of musketry, hence the name.

They were seldom over 10 cm high and had short, thick stems which were in one piece with the trumpet- or funnel-shaped bowls. The feet, which were wider than the bowls, were 5 cm or more in thickness to enable them to withstand the usage for which they were destined. They might either be solid with rounded edges, or straight-sided and with a downward flange. In the second half of the 18th century they were often listed by glass sellers as 'masons', but their use was not confined to the lodges. A figure in the foreground of Plate I of Hogarth's engravings of his Election series, published in 1755, is using precisely such a glass for drinking, and in view of the small capacity of the glass, the contents were presumably of a spirituous nature. Firing glasses were mostly plain, but they were sometimes engraved with fruiting vines, Masonic symbols such as a square and compasses, or, more rarely, with Jacobite emblems. *See* Ships' glasses.

Flashed glass: *See* Cased glass.

Flint glass: a name which has denoted colourless lead crystal ever since Ravenscroft (q.v.) used calcined flints as a source of silica, though they had been used in England at least a century before. *See* Harrison, William.

Flowered glasses: a contemporary description of glasses engraved with flowers, foliage or vines, from about 1740. This engraving was known as 'flowered work'.

Flute glasses: in British glass terminology the word 'flute' has two distinct meanings: first, a drinking glass of any size with a bowl which is narrow in relation to its height, and secondly, a design produced by cutting or moulding (*See* Fluting).

Flute glasses were made in large numbers in the Netherlands from the beginning of the 17th century, and their form conditioned that of a celebrated flute of probable English origin which was made in about

Flute, c. 1660

1660. This is the Scudamore flute preserved in the London Museum. It is in soda metal and about 37 cm high, consisting of a narrow conical bowl, with slightly concave sides, supported on a rudimentary stem comprising a hollow ball knop surmounted by a merese (q.v.). The wide circular foot is folded under all round the edge. The bowl is diamond-engraved with the arms of Charles II, presumably to celebrate the Restoration of the Monarchy, and those of the noted royalist, Viscount Scudamore. Such immense glasses were outmoded in Britain even in 1660, but the design influenced the style, if not the dimensions, of many of the more modest flutes of succeeding periods, to the practical exclusion of another 17th-century variety of different proportions.

This type, which has survived sparsely in both soda metal and lead crystal, consisted essentially of a tall, narrow beaker mounted directly on a round foot, the bowl being encircled by horizontal applied trails (*See* Mum). A hybrid between this and the Dutch style is represented by the Penruddock flute, now in the Corning Museum of Glass, New York State. This has a short, single-knop stem with a merese above and below, but the bowl, which also has horizontal trails, is wider at its base than the Scudamore flute and more like a beaker. It was probably one or other of these types that the poet Lovelace was alluding to in the mid-17th century when he mentioned 'Flutes of Canary'.

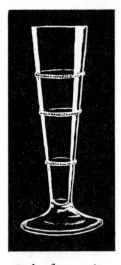

Beaker-flute, c. 1680

The Penruddock flute, c. 1680

A scale drawing of a flute was among the designs sent by the Glass Sellers' Company of London for the guidance of one of their suppliers, Morelli (q.v.) of Venice, early in the reign of Charles II and before the

Design for sack flute

advent of lead crystal. This glass, which was only about 16 cm high, had a straight-sided conical bowl and a short stem comprising a diminutive inverted baluster (q.v.) between two mereses. Although not an English glass, it is mentioned here for several reasons. First, its design was English, and it therefore provides evidence of the requirements of the contemporary English market; secondly, its proportions were echoed in many small British flutes of the late 17th and 18th centuries.

The latter are almost invariably classified by writers on glass and compilers of auctioneers' catalogues as ale glasses, but that this dogmatic appraisal has no universal warrant is evident from the fact that the Glass Sellers' Company's design, mentioned above, is clearly inscribed '1 Doz plain, 1 doz ribbed for sack'.

In these circumstances, it would be more reasonable to describe as ale glasses only those flutes which are engraved with hops and barley (q.v.), for it is highly probable that a plain flute would have been used for any liquor other than red wine, including sack, at the pleasure of the owner.

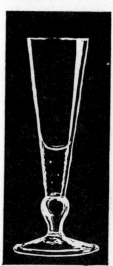

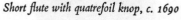

Short flute with quatrefoil knop, c. 1690   *Flute, c. 1685*

Many of these small flutes of the late 17th century had wrythen (twisted) ribs on the bowls, and the short stems often had the profile of an inverted baluster, but were pinched into four 'wings'. Surfaces became generally plain after 1730.

Meanwhile, from about 1680, taller flutes had begun to appear and were presumably made by Hawley Bishopp (q.v.), the successor of

George Ravenscroft. These lead flutes were over 21 cm high, but as the lower third or more of their conical bowls was solid glass, their capacity cannot have been much greater than that of the shorter flutes mentioned above. They simply looked more important and gained increased elegance from their height. Few have survived, but enough remain for us to know that the stems followed prevailing styles on glasses in general, and included at least the inverted baluster, the acorn knop, and the angular knop (q.q.v.), the first being the most pleasing.

After 1700, the bell-shaped bowl, which became an increasingly prevalent feature of other drinking glasses, began to appear in the attenuated proportions of the flute, and might be accompanied by the usual contemporary stem-formations such as the annulated knop (q.v.). At the same time, a subtle change began to occur in the relative proportions of the stem and bowl, with the former increasing in height at the expense of the latter, the capacity being maintained by making the bowl hollow down to its base in place of the solid glass of earlier examples.

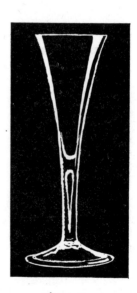

Flute, c. 1710   *Flute, c. 1735*

When plain stems appeared in the first quarter of the 18th century, many flutes displayed the same feature, often with elongated trumpet bowls. These and the bell-shape continued into the second half of the century, but in the 1740s, were joined by a long round-funnel, which was probably the most popular of all.

Meanwhile, air-twist (q.v.) stems were used on flutes as on other glasses from about 1730, and later on, were sometimes knopped; from about 1745, opaque-twists (q.v.) might form an alternative. The air-twists fell out of production in about 1760, but the opaque-twists persisted into the last quarter of the century. They ceased to be made in about 1780 owing to taxation, and thereafter, flutes with cut stems, which had existed coevally, had the luxury end of the trade entirely to themselves, with cut fluting (q.v.) tending to supersede faceting, and with plain stems continuing as a cheaper alternative.

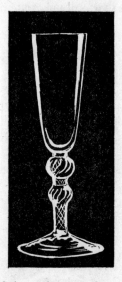 

Double-knopped air-twist flute, c. 1755   *Cut flute, c. 1760*

The bowls of flutes, which were mostly in a size suitable for wine, strong ale, or cider, and were sometimes engraved with appropriate motifs, also appeared in miniature form for cordials, chiefly with a round-funnel or conical shape which are usually associated, without conclusive evidence, with a cordial known as ratafia (q.v.). They might be plain, or engraved with flowers and vines or Jacobite motifs, which were sometimes found on normal flutes as well. Any of this surface ornament might be occasionally applied by means of enamelling (*See* Beilby).

Among the short-stemmed flutes, the straight-funnel, or conical bowl was a perennial favourite, but in the latter part of the 18th century, some of them might have elongated ovoid or U-shaped bowls. During this, the neo-classical phase, flute bowls of all kinds might be encircled, just below the rim, with a row of vertical incisions which were of Roman origin. They were usually accompanied by minute engraved sprigs and occurred on other kinds of contemporary glassware. At the turn of the century, the bowls of flutes often bore moulded fluting or moulded wrythen fluting, the latter presumably being imparted by giving the paraison (q.v.) a twist as it was withdrawn from the mould. Glasses of this kind continued to be made in the early 19th century when a number of other varieties, short, tall and of intermediate height, began to be produced as well.

Flute, c. 1780

Flute, c. 1800

Chief among these, in the high-class category, were flutes with funnel-shaped bowls, either quite straight or with a slight eversion of the rim, resting on a short stem with a bladed knop (q.v.) in the centre and a flatter protuberance at the junction of bowl and stem, usually in the form of two or three diminishing discs. Most of the bowls were cut with vertical fluting which rose to varying heights. These high-quality flutes, which were clearly the most popular of all in the Regency period, were made in three main sizes. The tallest, which were presumably intended for white wines including champagne, varied in height from about 22 cm at the beginning of the century to 17 cm slightly later. The intermediate size was just over 15 cm high, and the smallest about 14 cm. The author knows of a garniture of these three sizes still largely intact from the early 19th century. One could speculate endlessly as to their purpose, but it is clear that the differing capacity of such glasses, which were identical apart from their size, must be explained otherwise than by reference merely to champagne, cider, or strong ale, with the smallest providing a strong reminder of the 17th-century design marked 'for sack'. It is quite possible, in fact, that the smallest size was used for port.

The style in question was immensely popular, but others of the same period might have a small shoulder knop (q.v.), either plain or faceted, a true or inverted baluster stem, or a trumpet bowl merging into the stem in an unbroken line, with cut fluting rising from the base of the stem to part of the way up the bowl. The fluting was sometimes moulded instead of cut. A long bell-shaped bowl also occurred, but attracted little demand.

Other contemporary flutes were of less elegant appearance owing to their thick stems, which were borrowed from rummers (q.v.) of the

Flute, c. 1810

same period. The conical bowl rested on a merese. Beneath this, the short stem was either a stout cylinder, or a mere tapering upward extension of the foot, which might be circular, square, or polygonal. Most of these clumsier designs appear to have belonged in taverns, especially when they had deceptive bowls, but they were occasionally of such high quality, with carefully executed cut fluting, that these would seem to have been quite congruous with elegant domestic surroundings or inns of the better sort. ·

In conclusion, it should be remembered that a flute could be of any size and the bowl of any shape, providing that it was sufficiently tall in relation to its diameter.

Fluting: a flute, in addition to being a kind of drinking glass, is a straight-sided facet, formed by cutting or moulding, occurring in multiple form and named by analogy with the long, vertical hollows in the three original orders of classical columns, the Doric, Ionic and Corinthian. Moulded fluting began to occur on some glassware in the first half of the 18th century, and was common round the bases of Irish jugs and decanters after 1783. In the second half of the century it began to be executed by cutting. *See* Cut glass.

Fly-catchers: *See* Wasp catchers.

Folded foot: the foot of a stemmed glass object, which, in Britain, had the edge folded under, giving an extra thickness of glass all round the circumference.

Fruit baskets: there is a record of glass fruit baskets having been sold at Bristol in 1725, but their precise appearance must remain a matter of conjecture. Examples formed by pinching plastic glass threads together in an open mesh have survived from the late 18th century, but there is at present no means by which British specimens may be distinguished with certainty from those imported from the Netherlands. It seems evident, however, that many must be of British origin.

G

Gadget, or spring pontil: a spring-loaded clip on the end of a rod, introduced in the early 19th century and used to grip, for example, the foot of a drinking glass as an alternative to the pontil (q.v.). Evidence of its use may be deduced from the absence of any signs of a scar.

Gadroon (French, *godron*): raised ornament of classical origin consisting of a rib-like lobe of varying length, used in multiple form, sometimes alternating with flutes; chiefly prevalent in the late 17th and early 18th centuries and the early 19th century, and sometimes known as pillar moulding. *See* Cans.

Gaffer: an old name for the foreman or head of a glass-making team; possibly a remote corruption of 'godfather'.

Gatchell, Jonathan: succeeded John Hill of Stourbridge as directing intelligence of the Waterford (q.v.) glasshouse in 1786; he died in 1823 after consolidating Hill's pioneering success.

Gilding: the use of gold in the surface decoration of British glass artefacts has been noted as early as the late 16th century, some of the glasses of the Verzelini (q.v.) period having been embellished in this way. It was used on occasions throughout the 18th century, but did not wear well on glass objects which received much handling, so that there are often only faint signs of its one-time presence. It was used with great effect on blue glass of the second half of the century, particularly finger bowls and decanters (q.q.v.). Its use extended into the Victorian period.

Gimmel flask: a small double flask consisting generally of two miniature bladder-shaped bottles fused together, usually with their mouths pointing in opposite directions. It is uncertain when they were first introduced, but they have been known in Britain at least since about 1660. They were commonly used for oil and vinegar, and are sometimes difficult to date with any certainty.

Glass: the basic constituent of glass is silica, one of the most widely distributed elements in the world. Since its melting-point, however, is over 1720°C., it is only in comparatively recent times that it has been possible to make a special glass for scientific and technical purposes from silica alone. In ancient times, and for ordinary purposes at the present day, it has been necessary to employ, among other ingredients, an alkaline flux which has the effect of lowering the melting-point. When the making of glass vessels began in the Eastern Mediterranean in about the middle of the 2nd millennium B.C., the flux used was an oxide of soda, which occurred native in Egypt as a substance called natron. In Syria and elsewhere, the soda was recovered from the ash of certain burnt marine plants. One such plant, *salicornia*, grows on parts of the British coasts, its familiar name being 'glasswort'. Soda was the usual alkaline flux throughout the Roman Empire and later, in Venice, but inland glass-makers in Northern Europe used potash instead, obtained by burning wood such as beech, or ferns and bracken.

In his *Description of England* (1586), William Harrison wrote 'The poorest also will have glasse if they may; but sith the Venecian is somewhat too deere for them, they content themselves with such as are made at home of ferne and burned stone. . . .'

George Ravenscroft (q.v.) employed these time-honoured ingredients almost a century later in addition to lead oxide, his use of calcined flints as a source of silica being responsible for the introduction of the term 'flint glass', which is still used. The Venetians made use of quartz pebbles (*cogoli*) from the river Ticino, but sand was generally found more convenient later throughout the glass-making world.

Glass Excise Act: in August 1696, John Evelyn wrote in his diary: 'The Bank lending the £200,000 to pay the army in Flanders, that had done nothing against the enemy, had so exhausted the treasure of the nation, that one could not have borrowed money under 14 or 15 per cent on bills, or on Exchequer tallies under 30 per cent.' This financial crisis, brought about by an unprofitable Continental war, had been already looming the previous year, and in September 1695, a swingeing tax of 20 per cent had been imposed on flint glass, the perfected product

116

of an infant industry which had begun only in the reign of Charles II (*See* Ravenscroft). Manufacturers and retailers conducted such a vigorous agitation against this ruinous tax, that a Committee of the House of Commons eventually recommended its withdrawal, and it ceased to be imposed from 1 August 1699.

Thereafter, however, the industry flourished so mightily that taxation at length became inevitable, and the Glass Excise Act was passed in 1745 with effect from the following year. This tax was assessed on the raw materials, but cullet (q.v.) was immune from the provisions of the statute, so that by increasing the quantity added to the batch (q.v.), glass-makers were able to evade part of the effect.

This was eventually realized by the Exchequer, and a further Act of 1777 not only doubled the existing impost, but also embraced all the relevant materials including the tin-oxide enamel used for opaque-twists (q.v.). Statutes of 1781 and 1787 made matters worse, and a final Act of 1825 imposed a disastrous burden on the industry and also extended the legislation to Ireland, resulting, eventually, in the ruin of Irish glass-making. All this legislation was repealed in 1845, too late for the salvation of Waterford (q.v.).

Glass Sellers' Company: The Worshipful Company of Glass Sellers of London received an unratified Charter from Charles I in 1635 which lapsed during the Puritan dictatorship of 1649–60. A new Charter was granted by Charles II in 1664. *See* Greene, John.

Glory hole: the opening in an auxiliary furnace, to which a glass object in process of manufacture is taken to maintain it in a workable state, also to impart 'fire polish'.

Goblet: although this term was one of several applied in the medieval period to silver standing cups, it does not appear to have been used to denote a stemmed drinking glass until the late 18th century. It is now generally employed retrospectively to indicate a stemmed glass of unusually important aspect.

Greene, John: partner with Michael Measey in a London firm of glass sellers, Greene took an active part in the affairs of the Glass Sellers' Company in the reign of Charles II (1660–85) and was Master of the Company in 1679. Some of the correspondence between Greene and one of the Company's suppliers, Allesio Morelli of Venice, between 1667 and 1673, is preserved in the British Museum (Sloane 857). It is accompanied by scale drawings of many kinds of glassware, mostly drinking vessels, which were sent to Morelli for his guidance, and these designs of the Glass Sellers' Company provide interesting evidence of the styles which were in demand in London in the late 17th century. Relations with Morelli, though courteous, were unsatisfactory in a commercial sense, and it was chiefly for this reason that the Company decided to manufacture on their own account. This decision led to the employment of Ravenscroft (q.v.) and the creation of a flourishing native glass industry. Greene died in 1703, after witnessing the establishment of English lead crystal.

Greenwood, Frans (1680–1761): a distinguished Dutch glassengraver, probably of English origin, who applied his highly skilful decoration to Newcastle (q.v.) glasses in the 18th century. One such glass, stipple-engraved, is dated 1728 and is preserved in the Victoria and Albert Museum, London. He had previously engraved in line, the earliest dated example being of 1720. *See* Engraving, stipple.

Grog: a mixture of rum and water popular in the 18th and 19th centuries. It is said to derive its name from the fact that Admiral Vernon, who wore a grogram cloak and was accordingly known as 'Old Grog', ordered the dilution of the naval rum ration in 1740. No particular glasses were dedicated exclusively to grog, but rummers (q.v.) were considered as being among the more convenient.

H

Haedy: a German glass-cutter employed by John Akerman (q.v.) in the first half of the 18th century. He was probably the father of Christopher Haedy (q.v.).

Haedy, Christopher: a London glass seller, presumably the son of the Haedy who had worked for Akerman, and who travelled and sold his wares chiefly in South-West England in the second half of the 18th century. He advertised cut and engraved glass between 1769 and 1785, one advertisement in the *Bath Chronicle* of 1775 mentioning 'Curious barrel-shaped decanters cut on an entire new pattern'. *See* Decanters.

Harrison, William: in his *Description of England* (1586) Harrison provided proof of the fashionable esteem in which Venetian glass was held, and also of the existence of some kind of native manufacture. 'It is a world to see in these our daies, wherein gold and silver most aboundeth, how that our gentilitie as lothing those mettals (because of the plentie) do now generallie choose rather the Venice glasses, both for our wine and beere. . The poorest also will have glasse if they may; but sith the Venecian is somewhat too deere for them, they content themselves with such as are made at home of ferne and burned stone.'

Hill, John: a well known glass-maker of Stourbridge in Worcester-shire, who ran the Waterford (q.v.) glasshouse for the Penrose brothers from the time of its opening in 1783 until 1786.

Hobnail pattern: a cutting design of the early 19th century involving the further embellishment of a flat-topped diamond, the edges of which were bevelled. It occurred in two main forms. The simpler of these consisted of two diagonal incisions with a triangular-edged wheel, running into the corners of the diamond and forming a four-pointed star in intaglio. In the more elaborate version, two further incisions were made at right angles to the sides of the diamond, making an eight-pointed star. The term is often misapplied to other designs. *See* Cut glass.

Hollow shanks or stems: wide, hollow stems occurred on roemers (q.v.) of the late 17th century, but very seldom on glasses of any other kind. During the middle years of the 18th century, some plain, cylindrical stems on drinking glasses were occasionally hollow, but their incidence was never high. After 1830, the wide bowls of certain champagne glasses opened into the stems, probably to receive the sediment which was present before the introduction of the disgorging process, but these were never manufactured on a very large scale, possibly owing to the difficulty of keeping them clean.

Hollowed decanters: decanters with the rough scar left by the pontil (q.v.) ground off the base were advertised as 'hollowed' shortly after the middle of the 18th century, at a time when cut decoration was widespread. Thereafter, this form of finish was found on all decanters and jugs of good quality.

Hops and barley: ears of barley, either alone or with a hop-cone, leaves and tendrils, began to be used as an ornamental motif on glasses of many kinds intended for ale or beer, in the second quarter of the 18th century. This ornament was usually wheel-engraved, but was occasionally in white, vitreous enamel in the second half of the century (*See* Beilby). This decoration was not confined to the vessels of wine-glass size used for strong ale, which was as potent as wine, but appeared also on large cans or jugs (q.q.v.) with a capacity appropriate to small beer, which, while a product of the same ingredients, was of far lower alcoholic strength. *See* Ale or beer glasses.

Hyacinth glasses: *See* Bulb glasses.

Hyaloplastic: an adjective describing the decorative manipulation of glass otherwise than by blowing, applied, for example, to trailed and pincered ornament.

I

Ice decanters: a type of decanter, intended chiefly for champagne, with an internal ice-compartment which was filled from the outside, was known as an ice decanter. They were first advertised in 1755. *See* Decanters.

Incised twists: a form of stem treatment, current only for about fifteen years from the mid-18th century, consisting of closely-spaced spiral incisions on the outside of the stems of drinking glasses. Feet were very seldom folded, and the bowls were mainly of bell or round-funnel shape, often with slight moulded decoration. A fairly high proportion of such glasses were in green metal, which reinforces other evidence that many were exported to the Continent. The twists were coarse at first and thinner later. *See* Stems.

Inverted baluster

Inverted baluster: the inverted baluster was a stem-formation deriving from the architectural baluster, as found in balustrades, but with the protuberance at the top instead of the bottom. It was among the earliest forms to appear on stemmed objects after the introduction of lead crystal in 1675. Within the limits of the 17th century, the bowls of drinking glasses were always in direct or almost direct contact with the top of the baluster, but after 1700, subsidiary knops or a short length of stem intervened between the two parts, or the thick base of the bowl was manipulated to form a cyst (q.v.). The inverted baluster occurred in slimmer, lighter form from quite early in the 18th century, and appeared on and off thereafter up into the Regency period. *See* Stems.

Irish glass: at a time when the seeds of the Industrial Revolution were being sown in neighbouring wealthy Britain, Ireland was still a backward country owing chiefly to lack of material resources.

In the *Diary of a Young Lady of Fashion 1764 to 1765*, the diarist, Cleone Knox, recorded that, when staying at an Irish inn, 'Was woke up very early by a street cry below my window of *Dirty Butter for Servants!*'

Comical though this may seem, it connotes the open acceptance of abysmally low standards, and these arose from economic conditions in a badly-organized, agrarian economy. The Irish had a fine record of craftsmanship in many fields including manuscript-illumination and work in precious metals, and although the production of glass required no very costly raw materials, all Irish glass-making enterprises were bedevilled by a lack of supporting affluence in the home market, which rendered them vulnerable to circumstance. *See* Belfast, Cork, Dublin, and Waterford.

J

Jacobite glass: this is distinguished from other 18th-century glassware only by the presence of engraved, or very occasionally enamelled, designs relative to the Jacobite cause. The decoration probably all dates from after 1745, the year of the second rising in favour of the exiled Stuart dynasty, most of it being wheel-engraved.

One small group, however, was diamond-engraved with one or more verses of the Jacobite anthem, and as it ends with the word 'Amen', these glasses, of which only about two dozen have survived, are known as Amen glasses.

The complete anthem is as follows; the word 'soon' should be noted in the penultimate line of the first verse.

God save the King I pray
God bliss the King I pray
God save the King
Send him victorious
Happy and Glorious
Soon to reign over us
God save the King.

God bliss the Prince of Wales
The true born Prince of Wales
Sent us by Thee
Grant us one favour more
The King for to restore
As Thou hast done before the familie.

God save the Church I pray
and Bliss the Church I pray
Pure to remain
Against all Heresie
and Whigs hypocrisy
Who strive maliciously
Her to defame.

God bliss the Subjects all
and save both great and small
In every station
That will bring home the King
Who hath best right to reign
It is the only thing
Can save the nation.
                              Amen.

Slight ancillary ornament, often in the form of small running loops and flowers, occurred as well, and the crowned cypher of James II's son, whom the Jacobites regarded as King James III of England and VIII of Scotland. He died in Rome in 1766 after Jacobite activity in Britain had largely died down. Most of the Amen glasses had drawn cylindrical stems, sometimes with air-twists (q.v.).

Far more numerous than these were drinking glasses, decanters, and other objects, wheel-engraved with various arcane Jacobite symbols occurring either alone or in different combinations. Their meaning is entirely a matter of speculation, and glasses bearing them are attractive to collectors on account of their aesthetic merit rather than the significance of the emblems. These include the following designs. A large marine compass, often regarded as the badge of a club called 'The Cycle of the White Rose', a star, a rose with one or more buds, a thistle, sometimes growing from the same stem as the rose, a bee, a bird looking variously like a jay, a blackbird, or a snipe with dislocated cervical vertebrae, a lily of the valley, sometimes combined with a rather perfunctory rose, a butterfly and grub, an oak leaf, an oak tree, a spider's web, a daffodil, a carnation, caterpillars and larvae, a forget-me-not, a sunflower, and honeysuckle. An engraved portrait of Prince Charles Edward is occasionally found, though this motif and the rose design have been extensively forged since early in the 20th century. Laconic inscriptions in Latin are not infrequent, the commonest being *Fiat* (Let it happen), *Redeat* (Let him return), and *Audentior Ibo* (I shall advance more boldly).

Jacobite glass, c. 1750

Many of the drinking glasses bearing these symbols and sentiments had air-twist stems. The engraving was generally left matt, but the rose design often had parts of the centre of the flower polished. On glasses with facet-cut stems, however, the entire rose including leaves and buds was frequently polished, and although the effect is less striking than when the decoration is left rough from the wheel, some consolation may be gained from the fact that the polished versions have never received the attention of forgers, since there has never been the same demand for them.

Many cut glasses of the second half of the 18th century had short flutes spanning the junction of bowl and stem. This bridge-fluting, as it is called, was extremely common. If one looks into the bowl of such a glass, the rounded tops of the cut flutes have something of the appearance of petals; but the notion that this effect was conceived with the deliberate object of suggesting a Jacobite rose must be discounted.

Jacobs, Isaac: an important Bristol manufacturer of blue glass in the late 18th century who sometimes signed his work.

Jacobs, Lazarus: presumably the predecessor of Isaac Jacobs, Lazarus advertised as 'glass-maker to King George III'. He employed Michael Edkins (q.v.) in the 1780s as a gilder.

Jelly glasses: although jelly was sometimes served in wine glasses in the early 18th century and possibly later, glasses specially designed for this and other sweet concoctions were made from about 1680 onwards. The earliest were in the form of small rounded basins with folded rims: a feature which often occurred on other kinds of bowl; but in the early 18th century, a trumpet-shaped or funnel-shaped receptacle was used, with or without a handle or handles, and with a short stem.

Thereafter, the majority had bowls in the shape of a narrow bell, either true or waisted (q.v.), but some broadened out near the top in a pronounced fashion, possibly to provide room for a topping of cream. Bodies were either vertically-ribbed or plain. Most were of circular section, but a few hexagonal examples have been noted. Stems were either non-existent or rudimentary, the latter sort resting on domed or conical feet, the first being uncommon after the middle of the century. The feet were seldom folded, even in the earliest glasses.

Hyaloplastic treatment was frequent until the late 18th century, when it was usually replaced by moulded fluting (q.v.), though facet-cutting sometimes occurred from about 1750. From the first decade of the 19th century, jelly glasses might be cut with small relief diamonds or

Jelly glass, c. 1710

vertical fluting, and some tended to be slightly shorter and wider than 18th-century specimens. It seems possible that, at any period, they might sometimes have been used for drinking. *See* Salvers.

Joey: a colloquial name for a dram (spirit) glass, probably no earlier than the 19th century.

Johnson, Jerom(e): prominent London glass seller who was established in Duke Street by 1737, when he advertised 'all manner of cut glass'. In about 1740, he moved to the 'Intire Glass Shop' in the Strand, and carried on a highly successful business until after 1760. In 1742 he advertised 'diamond-cut and scalloped candlesticks', and also executed engraving in the form of fruiting vines and floral bands. Engraving and cutting were carried out in his own premises, and it seems probable that he had some business with the Continent, for, in an advertisement of 1757, he said 'All foreign commissions to be executed to the utmost care and perfection'. *See* Cut glass.

Jugs: this term has been applied to a wide variety of vessels whose only common feature is a single handle, including long-necked flasks of the 2nd and 3rd centuries which are structurally similar to certain handled decanters (q.v.) of the late 17th and 18th centuries. To confine the subject within reasonable bounds, therefore, we shall be concerned in this section only with the type of object which conforms to the general modern understanding of the term; that is to say, with the kind of vessel which might be described otherwise as a pitcher, and is provided with a shaped pouring-lip.

Although the type is of immense antiquity, British examples do not begin to survive in any numbers from before the late 18th century. They were made at least a hundred years before, and ribbed specimens

Jug, c. 1680

by Ravenscroft (q.v.) are still in existence. The basic design of these late 17th-century jugs, though not the surface-treatment, appears to have been influenced by silversmiths' work. The bodies are shaped some-what like an inverted helmet, the handles are twisted, and they are supported on short knopped stems and ribbed, circular feet. The rarity of such jugs and those of the first six decades of the 18th century must be explained otherwise than by the comparative fragility of the material. They were, of course, made singly, rather than in sets or pairs as in the case of drinking glasses and decanters respectively, and were, in any event, available in many other media including ceramics, pewter and silver, so that their manufacture was probably never on a relatively large scale.

Those without stems rested either on their own base or on a rim foot, and a baluster-shaped body enjoyed enduring popularity; but the fact has to be faced that no sort of complete typology can at present be established owing to lack of evidence.

In the second half of the 18th century, some jugs, often of comparatively small size, were made of white or blue opaque glass, or translucent blue glass, and it is known that these were among the items painted by Michael Edkins (q.v.) between 1762 and 1787. Many jugs in the characteristic striped or speckled glass were produced at Nailsea (q.v.) and elsewhere from the last decade of the 18th century, the manufacture of these and the blue and white versions extending beyond 1800.

These coloured wares, however, were unable to compete in volume with jugs made of colourless transparent metal from about 1770, when the neo-classical style, inaugurated chiefly by the Scottish architect Robert Adam after 1758, began in some degree to affect the forms of glassware. Examples from the earlier and more elegant part of this phase are greatly outnumbered by representatives of the burlier, more robust style which began in about 1780, and of which the Prussian-shaped decanter (q.v.) is an example, but some of them were among the most beautiful jugs ever made. They were tall and slim, and although their overall shape was often conditioned by the architectural baluster, their lower parts sometimes owed something to classical urns. These had rudimentary stems and were mounted on circular or square feet. The finest were cut all over with vertical fluting (q.v.) sometimes notched across the ridges, or incised with spaced, horizontal channels: a type of treatment found on the contemporary barrel-shaped decanters (q.v.) and many cruets (q.v.), which were virtually small jugs. Their attenuated form, while highly expressive of the prevailing stylistic idiom, also involved a sacrifice of stability, and mishaps arising from this circumstance may well have reduced the numbers of a type of jug which was probably never anything but expensive and uncommon.

The Cork and Waterford (q.q.v.) glasshouses, both of which opened in 1783, made extensive use of a shape which had appeared in Britain a few years earlier. The fact that this kind of jug often displayed, in its lower part, some affinity with the contemporary Prussian-shaped decanter was no accident, for jugs were frequently blown into decanter-moulds, but finished differently in the upper third above the shoulders. Some were plain, others had moulded fluting round the base, imparted by vertical ribs on the inside of the mould, but any of them were liable to be decorated by engraving with various kinds of simple ornament including hops and barley (q.v.) and inscriptions. It is doubtful if these vessels were intended for domestic surroundings of the more sophisticated kind, but the metal from which they were fashioned was often of superb quality, and they had a sort of stalwart sincerity which rendered them attractive.

Cork jug, c. 1790

Not all Irish jugs were blown into ribbed moulds, with or without the name of the factory in reversed letters inside the bases. This was the cheaper sort. Others were free-blown, with the disfiguring pontil mark ground off the hollowed base, and cut comb-fluting (q.v.) encircling the bottom. Some excellent jugs were made at Cork in the late 18th century, many of them being of a shape which, in miniature form, was popular among the Cork silversmiths for milk or cream jugs. The straight sides expanded upward from the base, then curved inward over the shoulders and out again to the pouring-lip on one side and the handle on the other. Between these features, the brim was slightly shaped by cutting. The body might be encircled by linked vesicas, that is to say, horizontal pointed ovals, or stars formed by radiating splits (q.v.). Just about the shoulders, a pattern often called the husk design frequently occurred. This consisted of a central, horizontal mitre-cut channel, with incisions on each side, sliced at an angle. In the late 18th century, this restrained cutting gave the glass jugs to which it was applied a more interesting appearance, without in any way vitiating the crystalline transparency of the metal.

Taller jugs, often cut with vertical flutes, continued to be produced extensively in the second quarter of the 19th century, but when cut decoration became generally more plethoric after 1800, the new designs such as sharp relief diamonds, which were typical of the Regency period, were applied most frequently to the squatter, broader jugs mentioned above, or modified versions of the same general design. In glass sellers' lists they were described as water jugs, and were intended for formal use at the dining-table.

To accommodate the deeper cutting demanded by Regency taste, a thicker, heavier crystal was essential, and in this connection, the Irish glasshouses were able to profit on an increased scale from their immunity from the provisions of the Glass Excise Act (q.v.), though it would be quite incorrect to suppose that all heavy, lavishly-cut jugs and other objects were made in Ireland. They were produced extensively in Britain, but were more expensive.

Increasing elaboration of cutting was a noticeable Regency characteristic, so that by 1820, it was unusual to find the body of a cut-glass jug with any appreciable plain surface left. All the contemporary patterns were called into service, with a predominance of sharp relief diamonds, and this form of decoration gave the glass a bristling appearance.

British glass had been linked by analogy with rock crystal since the 17th century, with transparency as its most desirable characteristic; but the numerous small reflecting surfaces on cut-glass jugs of the Regency show that this characteristic had ceased to be a primary consideration. Plain jugs continued to be made in large numbers for more humble environments, but the reason why these lacked the excessive cut decoration of their contemporaries, was not that this offended the aesthetic susceptibilities of their users, but that the heavier glass and extra work involved would have made them too expensive for the section of the market for which they were intended. Some, however, bore slight engraved ornament of various kinds, including, after the Battle of Trafalgar in 1805, commemorative portraits of Lord Nelson.

K

Kick: the domed hollow in the bases of some bottles, decanters, and other glass objects.

King glasses: a name applied before and after the Restoration of the Monarchy in 1660 to glasses engraved with the Royal arms and other emblems of loyalty to the Crown. Such glasses are now of great rarity. *See* Flute glasses.

Kit-Cat glass, c. 1710

Kit-Cat glasses: a widely misused term which should be applied only to a type of light glass of the early 18th century with a pointed round-funnel bowl (q.v.), a true baluster stem with a small compressed knop or torus at top and bottom, and a conical folded foot.

The name derives from a painting by Kneller in the National Portrait Gallery, London, of two members of a Whig political society, the Kit-Cat Club: Thomas Pelham-Holles, Duke of Newcastle, and Henry Clinton, Earl of Lincoln. Both sitters are shown with glasses of the sort described, and appear to be drinking champagne. It is possible that they were quietly celebrating the Duke of Newcastle's succession to the title, for his father was killed in a hunting accident in 1711, which is the approximate date of the picture. Many writers on glass and compilers of auctioneers' catalogues apply the name quite incorrectly to glasses with trumpet-shaped bowls.

Knops: decorative free protuberances on glass objects, typically on the stems of drinking glasses. The medieval phrase was 'knot', but the two words and the term 'knob' are all cognate. The following are the main forms in chronological order from about 1680. They are also described and illustrated separately under their respective names.

1680–1700: Inverted baluster, Drop knop, Ball knop, Angular knop, Double knop, Acorn knop.

From 1700: Ovoid knop, Annulated knop, True baluster, Mushroom knop, Cylinder knop.

Glasses of heavy construction embodying the above as dominant stem-features had fallen out of fashion by about 1725, but miniature or modified versions of many of these knops were liable to occur at any time afterwards. In about 1800 appeared the Bladed knop and the Annular knop, the first being a smaller, sharper rendering of the Angular knop already mentioned. *See* Stems.

L

Label decanters: from about 1755, decanters were sometimes engraved, or later, enamelled, with imitation bottle tickets bearing the name of the contents, such as Brandy, Rum, Shrub, Strong Ale, Port and so forth. Since the 1730s, silversmiths had been making bottle tickets, engraved or pierced with the names of various liquors including wines, which were hung round the necks of decanters by thin silver chains, and these chains were rendered in conventionalized form in the engraved or enamelled versions. Such decanters were known at the time as Label decanters. *See* Beilby.

Lace-makers' lamps: *See* Lamps.

Lamps: candle-lamps with glass sides began to be made in the second half of the 17th century, replacing the earlier lanthorns, the panes of which were made of horn; the old name continued, however, to be applied to them.

Oil-lamps followed in the early 18th century and were fashioned entirely from glass, apart from a metal lip round the aperture in the top from which the wick emerged. They consisted of a globular oil-reservoir mounted on a stem and foot, and often with a scrolled glass handle.

In about the middle of the century a larger type was introduced having something of the appearance of a cylindrical tea-pot. A wick-holder, either double or single, was opposite the handle, and others on each side. Although this new design gave more light – and burnt more oil – the older type persisted until quite late in the century, often taller than previously and with a foot like an inverted bell with a welted edge.

Mention must be made of what is known as a lace-maker's lamp. The term is often misapplied to a large globular glass vessel with a cylindrical neck and a foot, but this was not, in fact, a lamp at all. Filled with water, it merely served to concentrate the rays from a separate source of light on to the lace-maker's pillow or engraver's plate. The lamp itself might be of any existing type, or a candle might be used instead.

Laurence Vitrearius (Lawrence the Glass-maker): an immigrant glass-maker from Normandy, who settled at Dyer's Cross near Chiddingfold in Surrey in about 1226. His manufactory was primarily concerned with the production of window-glass, for which he received an order in about 1240 for Westminster Abbey, but it seems evident that he made vessel-glass as well. He was assisted by his son William, and succeeded so well that Chiddingfold was granted a Royal Charter in 1300. *See* Schurterre.

Lead glass: glass-of-lead or lead crystal was developed as a practical medium for glass vessels by Ravenscroft (q.v.) from 1675 when he first added lead oxide. The proportion of lead has always been approximately a third by weight. The resultant glass – or 'metal' as glass-makers call it – was far heavier than soda metal and took longer to set, but it was very ductile and had a power to disperse and refract light only slightly less than that of the diamond, which, in addition to its greater softness, rendered it particularly suitable for cutting in the 18th century.

It can easily be identified by a blue florescence in the presence of strong ultra-violet rays, like those emitted by a sun-lamp.

Leer: *See* Annealing.

Lemon-squeezer foot: a modern descriptive term applied to a type of foot found on rummers (q.v.) and other glass objects from about 1770. The hollow underneath, sometimes like the inside of a dome, was moulded with radial fluting (q.v.) or with alternate hollows and ridges of triangular section, which reflected light up through the glass.

Lemonade glasses: from the second half of the 18th century, hot lemonade was often served in small glass cans or mugs with single handles. The same kind of glass might also be used for punch (q.v.).

Light balusters: late in the reign of Queen Anne (1702–14) drinking glasses began to be made with stems of much the same shape as the pre-existing balusters (q.v.) but of altogether slighter proportions. An example is furnished by the Kit-Cat glass (q.v.). Many were made in two pieces, the stem being drawn from the base of the bowl. The most distinguished of all were made at Newcastle upon Tyne (q.v.) from the second quarter of the 18th century. *See* Stems.

Lillington, William: *See* Bowles, John.

Linen smoother: a heavy, mushroom-shaped glass object almost invariably in dark green metal, used for smoothing linen. The earliest were made in the first quarter of the 18th century.

London: by 1700, there were twenty-four glasshouses in and about London, which had been the fountain-head of national development since the time of Verzelini (q.v.) in the 16th century. By 1833, however, there were only three, one of which, the Whitefriars glasshouse, which had been founded near the Temple in 1681, is still in existence, though it moved to Wealdstone in Middlesex in 1922.

Lustres: a name which was applied for a time to chandeliers (q.v.), but which usually indicates small cut pendants.

Lynn (King's Lynn): Sir Robert Mansell (q.v.) had a glasshouse at Lynn in the first half of the 17th century, and another, a branch of a London enterprise, was there in 1693. It may have been the latter which was referred to as 'the glasshouse in Lynn' in a provincial advertisement in 1747, but it seems likely that it went out of business shortly after 1750.

Lynn is mentioned here because its name has long been associated with a particular kind of surface-treatment on mid-18th century glassware such as decanters and the bowls of drinking glasses. On the latter, of which surviving examples usually have opaque-twist (q.v.) stems, the bowl is encircled by shallow, horizontal grooves divided by low ridges which vary from two to seven in number. Many have folded feet: a rare and early feature with opaque-twists, since the majority were made after the Glass Excise Act of 1745 (q.v.) which discouraged the use of the extra glass involved in making the fold. On larger objects, such as the bodies of decanters, the grooves are wider and fewer. They are often described alternatively as 'Norwich rings', though there is no record indicating that a glasshouse ever existed in this ancient city.

M

Mallet-shaped decanter: a type of the first half of the 18th century, with almost horizontal shoulders and looking somewhat like a sculptor's mallet. It might be with or without a handle and have a body of circular, polygonal, or cruciform section. *See* Decanters.

Mansell, Sir Robert (1573–1656): retired Admiral and monopolist glass-maker. In 1611, five years before the death of Sir Jerome Bowes (q.v.), a licence to make glass was granted to Sir Edward Zouche and others, and Mansell joined the board of this firm in 1615. Pressure of business moved him to retire from the Navy in 1618, but he was recalled two years later to command an expedition against the Algerian corsairs. On his return, he persuaded his fellow directors at the Broad Street glasshouse to leave the board in an amicable fashion, and in 1623 obtained a patent from James I by which he took over Zouche's licence and was granted the right to make all kinds of glass 'with sea cole pitt coale or any other fewell whatsoever not being tymber or wood'. This proviso was in accordance with the *Proclamation touching glasses* of 1615, which banned the use of wood as an industrial fuel owing to the alarming spoliation of the forests.

Monopolies are now frowned upon, as they result in the elimination of healthy competition; but in the formative condition of British glass-making in the first half of the 17th century, Mansell's monopolistic position was almost certainly beneficial to the industry, for his financial skill and driving ambition led him to open new glasshouses or take over existing ones all over the country, including, in particular, Newcastle upon Tyne and Stourbridge (q.q.v.), both of which were destined to achieve eminence in the 18th century. In this way, the craft of glass-making was spread over a wide field, and the foundations of a national industry were laid. Mansell even gained control of a Scottish glass-house at Wemyss in Fifeshire in 1627, though this was not one of his more successful operations since its acquisition eventually involved him in serious financial loss.

As lead crystal had not yet been introduced, Mansell's productions were in soda metal, the barilla (q.v.) for which he imported in an organized fashion from Spain.

As British glass of the period was similar to that of Northern Europe in general and the Netherlands in particular, it is no easy matter to distinguish the many fragments and few complete specimens found in Britain from glass made elsewhere, on the mainland, at the same period. Some, however, must be Mansell's, though at the present state of our knowledge, no conclusive means of identification has yet been devised.

Marver: originally a marble slab on which the paraison (q.v.) was shaped by rolling and other motions, later made of smooth iron.

Mercury or mercurial twists: a sub-division of the air-twists (q.v.). The name, which is an apt modern descriptive term, arises from the fact that stems so described contain very broad air-spirals – usually no more than two – and these display a silvery brilliance reminiscent of mercury. They were introduced in about the middle of the 18th century, and have plain feet and usually trumpet-shaped bowls.

Merese: a narrow collar, sometimes with sharp edges, much used on stemmed glass objects of Venetian origin and Venetian style in the 17th century. It occurred to a trifling extent in Britain on glasses made of lead crystal after 1675, its incidence increasing in the 18th century, though it could not be described as a popular feature. It was sometimes found on early 19th-century rummers (q.v.) at the point where the bowl joined the stem.

Metal: the substance of glass in either a liquid or solid state.

Mixed twists: a combination of air-twists and opaque-twists (q.q.v.) in the same stem; occurring from about 1760.

Monteith (a); c. 1770

Monteith: (a) originally a silver bowl about 30 cm in diameter, in which wine glasses were cooled by suspending them by the feet through indentations in the rim, so that their bowls were immersed in cold water. The diarist Anthony à Wood, writing in *Life and Times* in 1683, stated that monteiths were introduced in that year and were named after a 'fantastickal Scot' who affected notches round the hem of his cloak or coat. The silver monteith, and a dual-purpose vessel with a detachable monteith rim which could be used otherwise as a punch-bowl, fell out of fashion in about 1720, but glass monteiths of similar proportions and with indented rims were made in the late 18th century.

'*Monteith*' (*b*); *c. 1800*

(b) A jargon term applied, for no apparent reason, to a small glass vessel mounted on a rudimentary stem and foot, often with a double-ogee bowl (q.v.), occurring in the late 18th and early 19th centuries. The type of glass to which this unsatisfactory epithet has become attached could have been used for dessert, salt, drinking, or general table purposes. It is also called a bonnet glass.

Morelli, Allesio: a celebrated Venetian glass-maker in the second half of the 17th century, and one of the most important suppliers of the Glass Sellers' Company (q.v.) of London prior to the introduction of lead crystal in 1675. It was Morelli's failure to make his glasses strong enough and supply them on sufficiently favourable terms, that eventually led the Glass Sellers' Company to encourage the creation of a domestic source of supply, and this led in turn to the establishment of a thriving national industry.

Mould-blown glass: known also as blown-moulded, this refers to a glass-making technique of immense antiquity, probably used from the 1st century B.C., when the blowing-tube (q.v.) was invented in Syria. The process consists of inserting the paraison (q.v.) into a mould, and blowing until it is sufficiently insufflated to press against the sides and bottom and thus receive its shape. Having once been introduced, the method never ceased to be used. Many decanters and jugs, for example, of the late 18th and 19th centuries, were mould-blown.

Moulded fluting: fluting (q.v.) imparted to a glass vessel by ribs on the inside of a mould.

Moulded pedestal stems: *See* Silesian stems.

Mugs: *See* Cans.

Mulvaney, Charles: *See* Dublin.

Mum: this was an unusual kind of beer brewed in Brunswick, and imported into Britain through Hamburg in large quantities from about 1660 until well into the 18th century. It was extremely potent, and sometimes contained unorthodox ingredients such as spruce, as well as being excessively bitter from the large amount of hop-resin in the wort. On 3 May 1664, Samuel Pepys recorded, 'I went to the Fleece, a mum-house in Leadenhall, and there drank mum'. In 1677 another commentator wrote: '. . . the mum at Brunswick is a medicine, and drinks very nauseous', its disgusting taste possibly convincing people of its therapeutic value. It seems to have had many devotees, and Henry Purcell wrote a catch about it in the reign of Charles II.

> *There's an odd sort of liquor new come from Hamborough,*
> *'Twill stitch a whole wappentake thorough and thorough.*
> *'Tis yellow and likewise as bitter as gall,*
> *As strong as six horses, coach and all.*
> *As I told you, 'twill make you as drunk as a drum,*
> *You'd fain know the name on't, but for that, my friend, Mumm!*

It is mentioned here because a particular sort of glass was evidently used to contain it, though one can only speculate as to its design. This is clear from the fact that in the late 17th and 18th centuries a colloquial name for the Monument in the City of London, commemorating the Great Fire of 1666, was 'the Mum Glass'. It may perhaps be deduced from this that such a glass was tall, straight-sided or very nearly so, narrow, and possibly with a cover, and the nearest contemporary British type was a long beaker or flute without a stem and mounted directly on a round foot. Similar glasses, such as the German *Humpen* or *Passglas*, may sometimes have been imported with the mum. It seems unlikely that there will ever be any very strong movement to resuscitate the beverage. *See* Flute glasses.

Mushroom knop

Mushroom knop: a bold protuberance occurring at the top of certain drinking-glass stems in the early 18th century, probably deriving from a similar turnery design on legged furniture of the 1690s. *See* Stems.

Mushroom stopper: a decanter-stopper shaped somewhat like a mushroom, used from about 1780, mostly in association with Prussian-shaped or cylindrical decanters. It sometimes had a small ball knop on the shank, especially in Waterford (q.v.). *See* Decanters.

Mustard-pots: mustard-pots of cut glass were fairly common in the late 18th and early 19th centuries, and were usually accommodated in the retaining-rings of cruet-frames together with casters (q.v.), though they have often become separated in the course of time. They were generally equipped with silver covers with a hole in one side for the spoon. The styles of cutting were typical of the period, and the date of any given specimen may be determined by an examination of the marks on the silver mounts, apart from the evidence afforded by the cutting-designs. *See* Cut glass.

N

Nailsea: a bottle and crown glass (q.v.) factory was opened in 1788 at Nailsea Heath, about eight miles from Bristol, by a bottle-manufacturer named John Lucas. Four or five years later he met Edward Homer who had an expert knowledge of vitreous enamel, and from this contact emerged the idea of making decorative glassware from bottle glass, which attracted far less tax than flint glass (q.v.).

Manufacture commenced in 1793, the partners being Lucas, William Chance, Homer, and William Coathupe, and met with such immediate success that glass-makers in Bristol, Sunderland, Warrington, Stourbridge, Newcastle upon Tyne and elsewhere at once began to turn out similar products.

The result is that it is now generally impossible to identify true Nailsea glass, but as other contemporary productions were of equal merit, the fact is of little importance, and the name 'Nailsea' has become a generic term for it all. It is difficult to take seriously as artistic craftsmanship, but some is undoubtedly attractive. It consisted of jugs, flasks, bottles, bowls, rolling pins, tobacco-pipes (non-functional), walking sticks, cans (q.v.) and so forth, mostly in dark green or black metal with stripes, whorls, or blotches of contrasting enamel, or a fine lattice-work in white or pink. Some of it is curiously reminiscent of early Venetian work without being identical. Production continued through most of the Victorian period, but the Nailsea glasshouse closed down in 1873, heavily in debt to its creditors.

Neck-rings: glass rings encircling the necks of decanters and carafes (q.q.v.) to provide a firm grip. They were introduced for this purpose

Neck-rings; round, square, triangular, double and triple

in the last quarter of the 18th century. The chief varieties are known as round, square, triangular, double and triple, the first being sometimes cut in the early 19th century.

Newcastle light baluster, c. 1730

Newcastle upon Tyne: although there was some glass-making activity in North-Eastern England three centuries before the Norman conquest, the first glasshouse to exist on Tyneside after the discovery of lead crystal was established in Newcastle in about 1684 by the three Dagnia brothers, sons of Edward Dagnia who owned a glasshouse in Bristol (*See* Dagnia). Coal had been mined in the area since the 13th century, and had been employed as fuel for glass-making before the Proclamation of 1615 rendered its use obligatory (*See* Mansell). The industry did not immediately achieve more than local success, but in the second quarter of the 18th century it began to produce, in addition to other kinds of glassware, stemmed drinking glasses of great distinction, fashioned from a metal of excellent quality.

In style and proportion, many of them were quite outside the confines of normal British development. The bowls, which consisted frequently of a round-funnel (q.v.) curving slightly outward, were generally larger than others, and the stems were taller and embodied light balusters and knops in a manner reminiscent of silver standing cups of the 1660s. A favourite device was to include small air-bubbles in the knops. It seems probable that these stylistic elements were introduced as a result of mercantile connections with Holland, where the Netherlandish version of the earlier *façon de Venise* often displayed many similar characteristics, without such glasses being identical in total aspect with those of Newcastle.

Newcastle glasses of the type in question are classified as light balusters, and were produced between about 1725 and 1780. They were quite different from the light balusters made in other centres. It was not long before they became an important item of trade with Holland, whose own glass industry had declined as a result of German and British competition after the Treaty of Utrecht of 1713, which concluded the War of the Spanish Succession. The Dutch, however, were highly skilled engravers, and found in Newcastle glasses an ideal field for their work. In the first place, they were imposing and elegant, and in the second place, the lead crystal of which they were made was considerably softer than Continental soda glass and therefore easier to engrave in either wheel-work or stipple (*See* Engraving). The glasses, the value of which was greatly enhanced by the engraving, were sold on the Continent and even re-exported to Britain.

One of the first of the relevant Dutch glass-engravers whose name has come down to us was Frans Greenwood (q.v.) of Rotterdam. A fine Newcastle glass engraved by him and dated 1728 is in the Victoria and Albert Museum, London. The stem consists of two balusters (q.v.), the lower true and the upper inverted, mounted on a domed and folded foot. The Newcastle dome was somewhat rounder than it was elsewhere. The bowl is stipple-engraved with a figure holding a roemer (q.v.), taken from a painting. The modelling seems almost miraculous. Another stipple-engraver of inferior skill was David Wolff (1732–98), who, like most of the Dutch engravers, used Newcastle glasses, while Jakob Sang was a wheel-engraver who signed glasses on which he worked between 1752 and 1762.

Newcastle light balusters, c. 1750

The light baluster style was apparently the most popular of all in Newcastle, but other types occurred as well, including plain, drawn trumpets, air-twists, opaque-twists, and cut stems. It is probable that many Jacobite glasses (q.v.) were made and engraved at Newcastle in the middle of the 18th century, fairly large numbers being in soda metal. Whatever the style, they were all of excellent quality, with the bowls displaying a smoothness which was unusual at the period, and a colourless clarity which shows that the technique of decolourizing (q.v.) had been throughly mastered.

Very occasionally, a glass of typical Newcastle form will be found to display a bluish tinge, arising from the inadvertent use of impure lead oxide; but such glasses are uncommon and the defect is largely redeemed by the crystalline character of the metal.

The more important Newcastle glasshouse was burnt down in 1782, but by 1811 there were no less than seven factories producing flint glass. The story of Newcastle glass in the late Georgian period is, however, that of British glass as a whole. A Newcastle glass-worker named Keith went to Norway in about 1750 to assist in a new glass industry at Nøstetangen. Not unnaturally, some of its subsequent productions were similar to those of Newcastle, but it is unlikely that many have found their way to Britain.

Nipt diamond waies: George Ravenscroft's description – and spelling – of a form of hyaloplastic (q.v.) ornament, which he applied to some of his glass vessels, consisting of a pinched raised pattern enclosing diamond-shaped spaces, the whole having the appearance of a net. This design had been used on Roman glass during the Empire, and in Venice in the 15th and 16th centuries. In Britain, it first appeared in the late 17th century, but was liable to recur from time to time during the century following. The pattern also occurred on mould-blown glass in the American colonies from about 1760, but with the addition of a conventionalized daisy-head filling each of the diamonds. *See* Ravenscroft.

Norwich rings: *See* Lynn.

O

Ogee bowl: a widely-used but slightly unsatisfactory modern name for a drinking-glass bowl, the sides of which, in the lower third, slope outwards from the top of the stem in the shape of a funnel, then change direction with a rounded angle to rise more or less vertically. Strictly speaking, an ogee is a low S-curve. *See* Bowls of glasses.

Opaque glass: 'opake' and 'composition' glass appear to have been terms applied from the 1740s to white glass of British manufacture containing tin-oxide enamel. The fabric itself had been familiar to British glass sellers at least since the third quarter of the 17th century, for an order of about 1668 sent to Morelli of Venice by John Greene (q.v.) of London, included a drawing of a covered vase of Chinese appearance, endorsed with the instruction, 'Must be made of your Milke whit glass & strong'. This vessel was clearly inspired by Oriental porcelain, as were many others made in Britain at a later date, the originals being known through importations by the East India Company, which received its Charter in 1600.

British opaque glass, whether white or blue, is sometimes considered inferior to British soft-paste porcelain as being a mere imitation of it, but this proposition is invalid. The Chelsea soft-paste factory did not begin operations until about 1745, whereas it is known from records cited by the late W. A. Thorpe that, by the early 1730s, exports from Britain to the American colonies included 'fine white Glass Japann'd', and 'Tea Setts of White, Blew and Japann'd Glass'. Furthermore, the Countess of Hertford wrote in 1743 that, in Southwark, glass had been brought 'nearly to resemble old white china.' It is evident from these facts that opaque glass was first in the field and may well have stimulated the English potters. 'Japanned', of course, meant painted in the Chinese manner, and was used in this sense in 1683 in connection with a set of chairs at Ham House near Richmond.

It is not certain when opaque white glass began to be made at Bristol (q.v.), but its production was well established by the middle of the 18th century. It was of superb quality and of a denseness which was hardly equalled anywhere else in Britain. It was to this fabric, and opaque blue, that Michael Edkins (q.v.) and other artists applied their painted decoration from the early 1760s. The tin-oxide enamel used in its preparation was also the raw material for the decorative spirals in opaque-twist (q.v.) stems.

Opaque-twists: spirals of vitreous enamel in the stems of various glass objects, especially drinking glasses, known also as enamel-twists and introduced in about 1745. The raw material was a composition of glass and white tin-oxide enamel, which was delivered to glass-makers in the form of bricks. This material was melted, and drawn out into long threads or sticks of varying thickness known as 'canes'. Short lengths of these were placed upright in grooves round the inside of a wide mould, which was then filled with molten glass. After cooling slightly, the whole mass was taken out of the mould and consisted, at this stage, of a thick cylinder of clear glass with the white canes embedded all round the outside. This was then re-heated and covered with another coating of glass, so that the canes were then enclosed within a larger cylinder. This was then drawn out and twisted by two operatives walking away from each other, until it was reduced to the required thickness, the canes increasing in length at the same rate as the glass in which they were enclosed and assuming a spiral formation. Short lengths cut from the resulting rod formed the stems for glasses.

Owing to the contrast between the transparency of the flint glass and the opacity of the enamel threads, the spiralling of the entire stem is seldom obvious; but if a thumbnail is passed down the outside, evidence of the twisting motion is often easily felt. The appearance and section of the enamel spirals were varied to create a wide range of effects.

The method simply described above produced what are known as single-series twists, but as double-series twists already existed with the air-twists (q.v.), they soon began to occur in enamel, and were made by placing various forms and arrangements of canes in the centre of the mould so that they drew out into a central column, with the outer twists spiralling round them. Over a hundred varieties have been noted and are designated by modern descriptive terms which are fairly easily comprehensible, such as spiral cable, spiral gauze and two-ply spiral band, multiple spiral twist, and so forth. The single-series opaque-twists were probably the earliest and are sometimes very effective, especially with knopped stems, but are outnumbered three to one by the double-series, for which there was evidently a greater demand.

For about fifteen years, opaque-twists were entirely white, but from about 1760, these might be mixed with air-twists, and from about 1765, might be in various colours such as blue, yellow, red and green, each of which was usually combined with plain white. Some colour-twists were in transparent flint glass, but these are less effective as the colour appears weaker owing to the transmission of light. The colours were made by adding metallic oxides.

Many glasses of various kinds with opaque-twist stems have survived, and they must have been extremely popular to compete successfully with cut stems, which began to appear on a significant scale at the same time. They fell out of general production in about 1780 owing to the Act of 1777, which not only doubled the duty imposed by the Glass Excise Act of 1745 (q.v.), but also levied a tax on the enamel from which the twists were made. Their almost total disappearance from glass sellers' ranges left the luxury section of the market completely open to the glass-cutters. *See* Cut glass and Stems.

Oppenheim, Mayer: London was the leading British centre for the manufacture of coloured flint glass in the mid-18th century, and a consignment of coloured glass smelling-bottles with cut decoration was sent in 1752 to Birmingham, where local glass-makers had presumably not begun to produce it. This and other transactions may have stimulated Mayer Oppenheim of the Snow Hill Glasshouse, Birmingham, to carry out his experiments, for shortly after the middle of the century he took out a patent for ruby-coloured flint glass. Unfortunately, none of his productions in this material has yet been identified, but he may well have initiated a tendency which culminated in the cased glass (q.v.) of the 19th century.

Overlaid or overlay glass: *See* Cased glass.

Oversewn foot: a drinking-glass foot of the middle decades of the 18th century, with applied thin, radial threads of glass running from the base of the stem outward over the edge; seldom found on any but dram glasses (q.v.). *See* Overstrung foot.

Ship's glass with overstrung foot, c. 1760

Overstrung foot: a drinking-glass foot similar to the over-sewn foot and of the same period, but with thicker radial trails more suggestive of string than thread.

Ovoid bowl: a bowl of a glass, of varying height and width, shaped somewhat like the more pointed end of an egg. *See* Bowls of glasses.

Ovoid knop

Ovoid knop: a shaped protuberance on the stem of an appropriate object such as a drinking glass in the rough shape of an egg, but often far more elongated, occurring to a limited extent at the beginning of the 18th century. Its scarcity may have been due to a certain lack of positiveness in its form, which appears to have been transitional between the ball knop of the late 17th century and the cylindrical knop of the first decade of the 18th century. It was almost invariably found with glasses of heavy construction, and is included terminologically among the balusters (q.v.). *See* Stems.

P

Paraison: the balloon of plastic glass on the end of the blowing-tube (q.v.).

Paste diamonds: imitation diamonds made of lead glass.

Paterae (singular: patera): oval or circular decorative motifs of classical origin, and part of the wide repertoire of neo-classical ornament popularized chiefly by Robert Adam in the second half of the 18th century, particularly the last quarter. The use of this ornament was widespread in the other applied arts, but appeared to only a limited extent in connection with glass, when it was usually engraved. *See* also Swags.

Pellatt, Apsley (1791–1863): distinguished London glass-maker. At about the time of his birth, his father, also Apsley Pellatt, commenced business at the Falcon Glass Works in Southwark, the firm's chief productions being cut glass (q.v.). The son began to take an active part in the business at an early age, his interests being artistic and scientific as well as commercial. He wrote two books on glass-making which were published in 1821 and 1849, but his considerable reputation stemmed chiefly from his successful manufacture of crystallo-ceramie (q.v.).

Penrose, William and George: two Irish gentlemen who were prime movers in the establishment of the celebrated glasshouse at Waterford (q.v.) in 1783.

Perrott, Humphrey: member of a glass-making family which had been engaged in the craft in Bristol since the late 17th century and was especially prominent in the 18th century. In 1735, Humphrey Perrott was granted a patent for an improved firing system on the same basic principal as a blast-furnace.

Piggin: a term sometimes applied to a covered or uncovered glass bowl with straight or curved sides and with one or two handles projecting vertically from the edge. Butter-dishes were sometimes of this form in the early 19th century.

Pillar moulding: an alternative name for gadroons, or sometimes, reeds (q.q.v.).

Plain stems: stems of drinking glasses without knops and consisting of simple cylinders. Glasses with such stems were made in large numbers from the early 18th century. *See* Stems.

Pococke, Dr Richard: mid-18th century author of *Travels Through England*, in which he commented on the contemporary glass industry. *See* Coloured glass.

Pontil or punty (Latin, *puntellum*): a solid iron rod about the same length as a blowing-tube (q.v.) used in the manufacture of glass vessels. Before the paraison (q.v.) could be detached from the blowing-tube so that it could be given its final shape, it had to be attached to something else. The pontil was put into the crucible of molten glass and a small gather picked up on the end. This was placed against the base of the object, to which it adhered on contact. A wet piece of cold iron such as a file was passed round the top of the vessel, which was then separated from the blowing-tube with a sharp tap on the iron. Shaping and trimming could then be carried out at the chair (q.v.). When the object was completed, the pontil was broken away from the base, leaving a scar known as a pontil or punty mark. This is to be seen on the feet of most drinking glasses up to the beginning of the 19th century.

After the middle of the 18th century, decanters and jugs (q.q.v.) of the best quality and a few cut drinking glasses had the scar ground off and polished, but it is always found on the cheaper mould-blown decanters and jugs made at Waterford, Cork (q.q.v.) and elsewhere. After 1800, it was almost invariably removed from the feet of cut glasses, but persisted on a great many others.

Pontil mark or punty mark: *See* Pontil or punty.

Port: a heavy dessert wine from the Alto Douro district of Portugal, fortified with brandy from the early 18th century, which began to be drunk to a modest extent in England in the second half of the 17th century, but gained great popularity after the Methuen Treaty of 1703, when Portuguese wines were subject to a third less duty than those of France. By the late 18th century, over three-quarters of the wine imported into Britain was from Portugal, and many port glasses of the period have survived to bear witness to its high incidence. Their purpose may be deduced from their capacity, which is comparable to that of similar glasses at the present day. In Scotland, where claret was the national drink, the introduction of port was resisted, but its consumption gradually increased after the Act of Union of 1707.

Posset pot or caudle cup: posset was a semi-liquid food, which was either drunk or eaten according to its viscosity, consisting of milk curdled with sweetened spiced ale or wine. Caudle was similar, but the basic ingredient was thin gruel instead of milk. Despite a complete absence of evidence that any specific glass vessel was ever dedicated exclusively to these concoctions, the names 'posset pot' and 'caudle cup' have often been applied in modern times to two distinct objects of the 17th century.

The first is a covered glass two-handled cup. Surviving examples are extremely rare compared with their counterparts in silver, which are relatively numerous. One such cup, made of lead crystal and dating from about 1685, belonged to the late Donald Beves of King's College, Cambridge, and has been illustrated by several authors. It bears the sort of hyaloplastic (q.v.) ornament which was fashionable at the period. The cylindrical body, curving inward at the base, is supported on a rim-foot. Short vertical gadroons (q.v.) alternating with flutes, encircle the lower part. Round the centre is an applied girdle with widely-spaced raspberry prunts (q.v.), and a pair of handles of Venetian type, one opposite the other, each shaped somewhat like a figure 3.

The domed cover has a large finial in the form of a crown surmounted by a cross, the whole object being 31 cm high. This imposing vessel, which was probably made by Hawley Bishopp (q.v.), has a monumental aspect which suggests that it spent most of its time standing on a piece of polished walnut or oak furniture in a decorative role, except when being used ceremonially as a loving cup on rare and special occasions. It is almost unbelievable that such a large and expensive vessel would have been intended for daily use as a container for posset or caudle, which would have left the inside covered with sour milk or gruel, necessitating its frequent washing.

Furthermore, a drawing of a smaller covered glass cup 18 cm high, with similar handles described by the designer as 'ears of good hansom fashion', appeared on an order of 1668 sent by the Glass Sellers' Company of London to Morelli of Venice. The caption to this design stated quite clearly that the cup depicted was for beer or wine.

It is surely more appropriate, therefore, that these glass utensils, like their relatives in silver, should be simply called 'covered two-handled cups': a name about which there can be no possible dispute and which cannot mislead anyone.

The other type of glass vessel frequently associated nowadays with posset or caudle is known otherwise as a 'spout pot' (q.v.). A similar utensil occurred also in silver in the 17th century, in the form either of a two-handled cup or a tankard (q.v.), with a swan-necked spout rising from near the base and tapering rapidly to an outward-curving mouth of very small diameter at about the level of the brim. This spout was so narrow that it would easily have become obstructed. In the glass versions, the spout was equidistant from the two handles, and the body might be plain, gadrooned round the base, or vertically-ribbed or fluted. It might also be U-shaped or in the form of a squat architectural baluster.

A reference of 1614, quoted by G. Bernard Hughes, mentions '1 skinker or a spout pot', from which it may be deduced that 'skinker' and 'spout pot' were synonymous terms. In old colloquial English, to skink meant to serve. Henry Purcell (1659–95) wrote a catch concerning a company of punch-drinkers, in which the idea that they would save time by helping themselves was expressed in the line 'We lose not a minute while we are our own skinkers'. At the end of the 18th century and possibly later, the youngest officer in a military mess was the skinker, it being his duty to 'wait on the company, ring the bell, stir the fire, and snuff the candles. . . .' The main purpose of a spout pot, therefore, was to serve liquor into smaller vessels. It is possible, of course, that metal or glass vessels of this kind were sometimes used for feeding infants or invalids as an alternative to a pap-boat, but there is no conclusive evidence to connect them specifically and exclusively with posset (or caudle). It would accordingly be far more reasonable to call them simply spout pots.

The few survivors are in both soda metal and lead crystal, one example having been made by George Ravenscroft (q.v.) in the reign of Charles II (1660–85). They appear to have fallen out of production in the early 18th century.

Potash glass: glass in which the alkaline flux is potash instead of soda.

It was obtained at least as early as the 16th century by burning wood, bracken or ferns, but is now added in the form of potassium chloride evolved chemically.

Pressed glass: the technique of press-moulding was developed in the United States in the 1820s as a cheaper alternative to hand-craftsmanship, and was introduced to Britain about ten years later. It was a means of mass production, but certain elaborate effects could not have been achieved in any other way. Many examples show an attempt to simulate cutting designs such as relief diamonds (q.v.) but only very rarely carry conviction.

Printies: circular or oval depressions made in glass with a round-edged cutting wheel. The design was of Roman origin and was added to the repertoire of British glass-cutters at the time of the classical revival in about 1770. It persisted into the 19th century, and even occurred from time to time on, for example, the shaft-and-globe decanters of the later Victorian period. *See* Cut glass.

Privateer glasses: during the Seven Years' War with France (1757–1763), British privateers often operated against French shipping. Glasses were sometimes engraved in reference to these privately-financed warships, usually depicting the vessel, with some kind of inscription such as 'Success to the Lyon Privateer', 'Success to the Eagle Frigate', and so forth. The glasses themselves were typical of the period and, like other commemorative glasses and Jacobite glasses (q.v.) were distinguished only by the engraving.

Prunts: blobs of glass, applied to many objects from the late 17th century, either plain or comprising circular clusters of minute hemispheres. The latter are known as raspberry or strawberry prunts, and commonly occurred on the wide, hollow stem of a type of glass called a roemer (q.v.). In this connection, the prunts were functional as well as decorative, for they improved the grip. They fell out of favour with other kinds of hyaloplastic details in the early 18th century. *See* Roemer.

Prussian-shaped decanter: a type introduced in about 1780, with a squat body shaped somewhat like a cask, and a neck which was normally embellished with from two to four neck-rings to provide a firm grip. The Prussian-shaped decanter appears to have been the first type made at Waterford by English craftsmen from 1783. *See* Decanters.

Pucellas: a pair of tongs used for shaping parts of glass objects while the metal was in a plastic state. After the pontil (q.v.) had been attached to the foot of a drinking glass, for example, and the incipient bowl had been separated from the blowing-tube, it still had a semi-balloon shape which had to be modified. This was done by rolling the pontil along the arms of the chair (q.v.) with one hand, while the other hand manipulated the pucellas, one arm of which was inside, and the other outside, the bowl. Up to about the middle of the 18th century, the pucellas was made of metal, and slight checks in the rolling motion or momentarily increased pressure sometimes left vertical marks in the glass. The tool was then more frequently made of wood, which tended to produce a smoother surface.

Punch: *See* Punch-bowls.

Punch-bowls: ceramic bowls were used for the brewing of punch soon after it was introduced into Britain in about 1630 by Englishmen returning from the Orient, and silver punch-bowls from about 1660; but these vessels do not appear to have been made of glass until after 1680.

The name of the drink derives ultimately from a Sanskrit word *pañca*, meaning five, with reference to the number of essential ingredients: water, spirit, sugar, spices and limes or lemons. The spirit generally consisted of brandy for some years.

Glass punch-bowls of the late 17th century were sometimes in the form of large, covered roemers (q.v.), mounted on stems and feet, but these were wholly superseded by bowls of normal type, about 30 cm in diameter, after 1700. Owing to the obvious likelihood of a high casualty-rate, it is difficult to assess their incidence throughout the 18th century, but bowls made of china, pewter, or silver were clearly more suitable and were probably more numerous. In the early 19th century, glass punch-bowls were often of very large size, and were sometimes accompanied by a glass ladle and glass cups.

Punts: minute oval or circular depressions, like miniature printies (q.v.), cut in the surface of glass with a small wheel. They frequently occurred round the tops of bowls of cut glasses in the second half of the 18th century, often accompanied by tiny sprigs cut with an engraving wheel. *See* Cut glass.

Punty: *See* Pontil.

Pyramids: glass salvers arranged to form pyramids, diminishing upwards in size. *See* Salvers.

Q

Quatrefoil knop

Quatrefoil knop: a stem-formation found mostly on drinking glasses of the late 17th century, but occasionally on jugs as well, consisting of a protuberance pinched into four narrow, vertical lobes, the sides of which were often impressed with cross-hatching; sometimes called a winged knop.

R

Ratafia: an alcoholic fruit-cordial popular among ladies for most of the second half of the 18th century. It is mentioned here because it is widely assumed that a particular sort of glass was reserved exclusively for it.

This glass was a small, slender flute with either a round-funnel or straight-funnel bowl (q.q.v.) no more than 2.5 cm in diameter at the rim. These bowls usually bore engraved decoration. Stems were mostly cylindrical, and might be of plain, air-twist, or opaque-twist type (q.q.v.). The feet were always plain, which indicates that these glasses appeared after the Glass Excise Act (q.v.) of 1745. So far as the author is aware, the only piece of evidence linking them with ratafia is in the fact that they are still sometimes used for this rather weak cordial in France at the present day and may have been devoted to the same purpose in the 18th century; but even if this is so, it cannot be assumed that a French convention was universally accepted in Britain. These dainty little flutes, which are extremely attractive, are very seldom encountered, and none has been found with a cut stem. *See* Flute glasses and Cordial glasses.

Ravenscroft, George (1618–81): a retired ship-owner and an educated man with a taste for experimentation in glass technology, at a period when scientific enquiry was being fostered by the interests of King Charles II, who gave a Charter to the Royal Society in 1662.

Ravenscroft's close association with the influential Glass Sellers' Company of London arose largely from the failure of one of the Company's chief suppliers, Allesio Morelli (q.v.) of Murano in the lagoon of Venice, to make his drinking glasses, in particular, strong enough to satisfy the requirements of the London market. In May 1671, John Greene (q.v.) on behalf of the Company, wrote to Morelli as follows: 'Sir, I praij you once againe to take such care that I may have good (glasses) and be used verj kindlj in the prices, else it will not be to my Interest to send to Venice for neither drinking glasses nor Lookeing glasses, for we make now verij Good Drinking Glasses in England and better Lookeing Glasses than any that comes from Venice'.

Whether or not the last statement was strictly correct is a matter of conjecture, but what is abundantly clear is that the Company had reached a point where it was willing to seek an alternative source of supply. They soon had their eye on Ravenscroft. In 1673, he built a glasshouse on the left bank of the Thames at the Savoy, and after experimenting for some months, applied for a patent for 'a particular sort of Christalline glass'. While the application was pending, the Company entered into an agreement with him in April 1674 by which he undertook to supply them with part of his production. The patent was granted the following month, and this emboldened the Company to make a second agreement in September 1674 appointing Ravenscroft their official glass-maker who would place his entire output at their disposal. They also enabled him to erect an experimental glasshouse at Henley-on-Thames, away from the prying eyes of commercial rivals outside the Company.

For some time, in addition to the silica, which consisted of sand and calcined flints reduced to the consistency of flour, he used an excessive quantity of alkaline flux, which produced an effect known as Crizzling (or crisseling) (q.v.). When this was present, the metal appeared to be filled with thousands of strands of floss silk, and in bad cases, the disease was progressive, causing eventually a bleak, whitish opacity as though the object concerned were filled with a dense fog. Dr Robert Plot, who visited Ravenscroft's glasshouse, described crizzling as 'a Scabrities or dull roughness irrecoverably clouding the transparency of the glass'.

It appears that, in 1675, Ravenscroft added lead oxide in place of some of the silica with the object of curing the defect. It is not known why it occurred to him to do so, but the idea may have been suggested by the use of lead as a glaze for ceramics. In the event, although the difficulty was not wholly overcome, his decision was momentous, for it marked the imminent birth of British lead crystal.

All seemed to be going well, and in June 1676, the Glass Sellers' Company issued a certificate of quality in the following terms: 'Wee the under written doe certify and attest that the defect of the flint glasses (which were formerly observed to crissel and decay) hath been redressed severall months agoe and the glasses since made have all proved durable and lasting as any glasses whatsoever. Moreover that the usual tryalls wherewith the essay of glasses are made have been often reitterated on these new flint glasses with entire success and easy to be done againe by any body, which proofs the former glass would not undergoe, besides ye distinction of sound discernible by any person whatsoever'.

The 'distinction of sound' referred, of course, to the resonant, bell-like note given out by a lead glass of suitable shape when struck: an effect which no soda glass could match.

In May 1677, Ravenscroft began to apply a seal to his glasses in the form of a raven's head, taken from his own armorials, impressed in relief on a small pad of glass, and these sealed glasses continued to be sold until 1681, when Ravenscroft died. A few have survived, and the fact that many of them are crizzled shows that the Company's certificate was premature, though the necrological process probably did not manifest itself nearly as quickly as with the earlier glasses. It was cured completely by Hawley Bishopp (q.v.) who added a higher proportion of lead oxide, but the credit for inventing glass-of-lead must go to George Ravenscroft, for it was his striving, failing, and striving again until he attained apparent perfection that made its final development possible.

The categories of glass objects to which surviving sealed examples belong are jugs, bowls, decanters, cans and roemers (q.q.v.), but certain unsealed specimens of the period, both crizzled and uncrizzled, may well have been made by Ravenscroft also. *See* Lead glass.

Reeding: series of convex pilasters of approximately semi-circular section and varying width, named by analogy with reeds laid side by side. Reeding was almost invariably vertical, and often occurred, in particular, on the bodies of certain cylindrical decanters of the late Regency (q.v.) period. It was mostly produced by blowing the paraison (q.v.) into a mould with internal vertical grooves, but appears on occasion to have been formed by cutting. Reeds are sometimes indistinguishable from gadroons (q.v.), but tend to be straighter and with parallel or almost parallel sides. They are the exact opposite of flutes, which are concave. *See* Fluting and Cut glass.

Regency: the historic Regency began in 1811, when George, Prince of Wales, was appointed Regent to perform the duties of King George III who had become hopelessly insane. It terminated in 1820 when the old King died, and the Regent ascended the throne as George IV. In a stylistic sense, however, the term is applied to the period from 1800 to about 1830, though certain elements of the style persisted into the early Victorian era. *See* Cut glass, Flute glasses, and Rummers.

Relief diamonds: a cutting design which existed in two versions. (a) Diamonds cut in very low relief with a mitre-wheel having an obtuse-angled edge, so that the degree of projection was minimal and scarcely perceptible in the profile. This version, which first appeared in the second quarter of the 18th century, enlivened the surface of the glass without reducing its transparency. (b) Smaller, sharper diamonds of pyramidal form, cut with a narrower wheel with the edge in the shape of a more acute angle. These began to become popular in about 1800, and were used modestly at first in small fields. As the aesthetic climate changed, however, and the graceful elegance of the Adam style gave way to the coarser fulsomeness of the Regency, they were used more extensively, so that large areas of glass were covered with small reflecting surfaces. Both kinds were formed by cutting opposed channels of V-section more or less at right-angles to each other. *See* Cut glass.

Rodneys: *See* Ships' decanters.

Roemer by Ravenscroft, c. 1680

Roemer or Römer: a German word meaning 'Roman', which is also a noun denoting a kind of drinking glass with a bowl which approaches the form of a sphere with a slice cut off the top, and a wide, hollow stem usually embellished with raspberry prunts (q.v.). These glasses were popular in the Habsburg Empire from the 16th century and may have been Roman in origin; the shape was certainly known in Anglo-Saxon England, for an example in an unknown material is shown in an English manuscript of the 11th century. Many of excellent quality were made in the Netherlands in the 17th century, usually in green glass, and there was evidently a demand for them in Britain in the second half of the 17th century, for they figured among various kinds of glasses ordered from Venice by the Glass Sellers' Company of London (q.v.).

George Ravenscroft (q.v.) produced some roemers in colourless lead crystal in the reign of Charles II, but since, so far as is known, only two have survived, it is impossible to assess their incidence, though a few others exist without the raven's head seal. One fine sealed example is in the Victoria and Albert Museum, London, and has a vertically-ribbed bowl which bears witness to Ravenscroft's delight in his new metal. The amount of crizzling (q.v.) is trifling and the glass is truly crystalline in character. The stem has the usual raspberry prunts, but in place of one of them is a pad of glass bearing the raven's head seal. It is 16.5 cm high. The other, in private possession, has a bowl with a raised trellis pattern which Ravenscroft called 'nipt diamond waies' (q.v.).

Some were made in the 18th century with narrower, and sometimes solid, stems, though these departed so much from the original design that it is barely justifiable to include them in the same category.

The roemer form was not confined entirely to drinking glasses for Rhenish and other white wines. It also appeared occasionally in the late 17th century in gigantic versions with covers, which were intended as punch-bowls.

The common contemporary English corruption of the name was 'rummer', though it was sometimes spelt 'romer' without the *Umlaut*; but it is convenient to keep the original German term for the type under discussion, as the word 'rummer' was applied in the 18th and 19th centuries to glasses of an entirely different character.

Rolling-pins: glass rolling-pins began to be made in the last decade of the 18th century, though the extent to which they were used for their ostensible purpose instead of being hung on the wall as ornaments is a matter of conjecture. Few examples were dated, and as they continued to be made into the second half of the 19th century, it is seldom possible to assign a given specimen to its period of origin with any certainty.

Rolling-pin, c. 1800

Most of them were about 37 cm long with a knob at each end. These knobs provided an anchorage for the string by which they were suspended, and one of them usually had a hole in it, with a stopper or cork, which has led to the reasonable belief that plainer examples served as containers for salt, tea, or anything else considered suitable by the owner. Many, however, bore decoration of various kinds, and in view of the risk involved in putting such cherished objects to constant use, it seems likely that these generally remained hanging on the wall.

They occurred in many kinds of glass: dark green, colourless, opaque white, blue, painted or enamelled in colour, and striped or blotched in the style associated with Nailsea (q.v.). Some of them had inscriptions in gold, enamel or paint, mostly of a sentimental nature, such as *Be true to me*, while others gave evidence of nautical associations; but the widespread belief that they were all intended as gifts from sailors to their sweethearts or from girls to sailors is certainly unfounded. Other objects such as glass walking sticks, tobacco-pipes, and swords were common elements of country fairs in the late Georgian period, and glass rolling-pins merely provided an alternative to these.

Round-funnel bowl: the bowl of a drinking glass with a rounded base and straight sides widening to the rim. *See* Bowls of glasses.

Ruby glass: *See* Oppenheim.

Rummers: the true roemer (q.v.) quickly lost any popularity it may have had by the early 18th century, but from this time onward, the normal English corruption of the term, 'rummer', was applied to any kind of stemmed drinking glass with a bowl which was large in relation to the other parts and noticeably dominated the design. It had, of course, nothing to do with rum. Many taverns were called 'The Rummer', and their signboards, which were sometimes depicted in contemporary engravings by Hogarth and others, showed large vessels of somewhat indeterminate character, but which were seldom anything like the German originals. It is evident from this fact and the few extant goblets which display some affinity with the pictorial representations, that the word had changed its meaning, but we have to wait until the neo-classical style began to become widely accepted in about 1770, for it to gain new authority from being applied to objects of a more positive character, which were manufactured on an increasingly large scale.

Rummer, c. 1780

These rummers, which have survived in considerable numbers, owed nothing to the 17th-century roemer, but derived with some fidelity from classical originals, in various materials including silver and glass, which were discovered in the excavations of Herculaneum and Pompeii (*See* Adam). They were made in a large range of sizes, from gigantic specimens used for serving toddy by means of miniature ladles or toddy-lifters (q.v.), to small dram glasses for spirits.

The most popular held something under half a pint, and were more numerous than the others because of their general utility; but it is not size which qualifies a glass for inclusion among the rummers, but proportions.

The earliest had ovoid bowls (q.v.) made in one piece with the stems, which were very short, and feet might be circular, square, or occasionally polygonal. The round-footed type was the commonest and looked like an enlarged version of an ordinary china egg-cup. Some were entirely plain, but the bowls of most of them were decorated with moulded fluting (q.v.) in the lower half, while a few of superior quality had cut fluting, which never extended down the stems within the limits of the 18th century. Above the moulded flutes, the bowl was sometimes encircled, just below the rim, by rather poor, shallow engraving in the form of swags (q.v.), knots, and so forth, as a further concession to neo-classicism, but was seldom executed with anything approaching doctrinaire exactitude. The general impression, in fact, is that these glasses did not belong in a formal, elegant setting; but the cut rummers were another matter.

The two-piece rummer with ovoid bowl remained widely popular up to the end of the 18th century, but in the last decade, a three-piece

Rummer, c. 1800

version, with bowl, stem and foot made separately and welded together, was offered as a more expensive alternative. The bowl was still ovoid,

164

but a compressed spherical knop was often positioned immediately below it. The lower half of the bowl might be embellished with cut fluting, but other designs, also of classical origin, were sometimes used instead. They included rows of vertical incisions known as 'splits', which ran round the top and bottom, sometimes with printies (q.v.) between. When such a rummer had a square foot it was fairly thin and flat with polished edges. The pontil mark (q.v.) was removed from the base, which might then be cut with a star consisting of splits radiating from the centre. The metal was usually of superb quality.

In the last years of the century, the bucket-shaped bowl, which had been used on and off for about a hundred and fifty years, appeared in the proportions appropriate to the rummer, and was destined to be one of the most popular forms of the Regency (q.v.) period. The short stem on which it was supported frequently had a bladed knop (q.v.) in the centre, while the moulded foot was very often square and surmounted by a hollow dome with radiating flutes or channels of V-section underneath which reflected light up through the glass. This type of foot is now usually described as a 'lemon-squeezer' foot (q.v.), and occurred at the same period on other items such as candlesticks and salts.

Ovoid rummers with feet of various kinds persisted to some extent into the 19th century, often cut in a manner typical of the period (*See* Cut glass); but in about 1800, a little variety was introduced in the form of a collar or merese (q.v.) at the base of the bowl and the top of the stem, which serves to distinguish many of these later glasses from those of the 18th century when other details are identical. Occasionally, the stem was cut with flutes.

One type with an ovoid bowl but often without the merese, had a stem which was a mere narrowing, upward extension of the foot, a similar formation being found on certain flute glasses (q.v.) at the same time. This stem was seldom of circular section, and consisted generally of a truncated square-section pyramid with concave sides. Yet another kind had a square foot crowned by a solid dome without the 'lemon-squeezer' below, and terraced on the outside.

In the early 19th century, rummers with bucket-shaped bowls became immensely prevalent, and were often of such high quality that it may be assumed that they found a place in formal table-settings. Like many other varieties, they occurred in different sizes, those of medium capacity being advertised simply as 'wines'. The feet were mostly round, with the pontil mark ground off the base leaving a polished depression. The short stem usually had a bladed knop in the centre, and

Rummer, c. 1810   *Rummer, c. 1815*

Rummer, c. 1815

several reinforcing discs occurred where it joined the base of the bowl. The latter was most frequently cut with vertical flutes.

Two other bowls of the Regency period seldom bore any cut decoration, though like their fellows, they might sometimes be engraved. One was of a kind of double-ogee (q.v.) shape, usually with a flattish base. These rummers are sometimes mistaken for modern glasses, but the metal is generally slightly darker and a pontil mark is almost invariably present under the foot.

The other type, which was supported on a thick, cylindrical stem with a merese at the top, had straight sides which expanded upward but changed direction a short distance below the rim. They either curved upward and rose more or less vertically, or broadened out slightly before doing so.

Late in the Regency, a rummer with a plain, flat-based cylindrical bowl began to be made in large numbers, and together with a round-based version like a tall letter U, continued to be manufactured up to about the middle of the 19th century.

S

Sack: a heavy, fruity wine from the Iberian Peninsula known in Britain from the late Middle Ages. The origin of the name is obscure, being derived by some from the Spanish word *seco*, dry, and by others from *saco*, a kind of wine-skin. When the wine concerned was actually from Jerez de la Frontera it was sometimes called 'sherris sack', but it seems likely that the word used by itself was often a mere generic term for many wines of the same character. Sack glasses, which were of different types and were generally of smaller capacity than those used for claret and other beverage wines, were mostly of no particular shape; but in the second half of the 17th century, short flute glasses (q.v.), associated by many writers exclusively with strong ale, were sometimes used for sack, and this usage may well have persisted.

Salad bowls: *See* Bowls.

Salt-cellars: this term is, strictly speaking, inherently tautological, since 'cellar', in this connection, derives from the Latin *salerium*, a salt-container; throughout the Middle Ages and well into the 18th century, such an object was always known simply as a salt, and often appeared under this name in old inventories. Small silver salt-cellars, now usually called 'trencher salts' for no apparent reason, first appeared in appreciable quantities after the Restoration of the Monarchy in 1660, at a time when the great standing salt, having lost its medieval social significance, had disappeared from domestic surroundings and performed only a ceremonial and ostentatious role among official bodies such as City livery companies. An absence of early examples makes it impossible to determine whether small glass salts were made at the same time, though it seems likely that they did not come on the scene until the early 18th century.

In 1724, 'glass salts' were mentioned in an advertisement without any qualifying phrases, suggesting that they were something new, and it is probable that they followed contemporary silver forms, without, of course, their angular precision, since glass can be worked cold only by abrasion. The silver salts of the period were low, with flat external bases, and of circular, polygonal, or oblong shape, sometimes with re-entrant corners, and the glass versions were presumably simplified renderings of these. For two decades from about 1720, a type of silver salt, consisting of a low, round bowl mounted on a circular foot, enjoyed some popularity, and may have provided part of the inspiration for later glass salts supported on stems and feet. But there is no doubt about the origin of circular examples of glass with outward-curving sides, standing on three short legs somewhat like the cabriole legs on contemporary furniture. They were copied as closely as the different medium would permit from silver salt-cellars of similar design which began to become popular in about 1740. At the point of attachment of each leg to the body, there might be either a simple outward bulge or moulded ornament such as a lion's mask, while the foot itself was commonly incised to suggest a paw. All these details were found on the furniture-legs of the pre-Chippendale era, and accorded with the style associated with the name of the architect William Kent. These attractive objects remained fashionable far into the second half of the 18th century, some being made of opaque white glass; but that several styles existed at the same time is evident from an advertisement of 1752 which referred to 'salts with and without feet', though whether 'feet' meant the short legs mentioned above, or the

Salt, c. 1740

circular feet on the stemmed salts already alluded to is difficult to determine.

Circular salts on knopped or unknopped stems and feet were often cut with hollow diamond facets from about 1750, and sometimes had scalloped edges, but when the neo-classical style, inaugurated chiefly by Robert Adam (q.v.), became practically universal in about 1770, these were generally superseded by boat-shaped salts on short stems and diamond-shaped feet, often with the 'lemon-squeezer' (q.v.) formation underneath which occurred on many contemporary rummers (q.v.) and other objects. The downward-spreading stems of these salt-cellars,

Salt, c. 1790

which have survived in comparatively large numbers, were usually cut with broad fluting (q.v.), while the bowls, which might have plain or scalloped edges, were cut with designs such as low-relief diamonds which were found on other glassware of the late 18th century.

The type under discussion persisted into the Regency (q.v.), the period being often deducible from the cutting designs. In the Irish glasshouses of Waterford and Cork (q.q.v.), some salt-cellars of the late 18th and early 19th centuries were like miniature versions of certain standing bowls, and were not only mounted on stems and feet, but also had turned-over rims. In the 1820s, large numbers of somewhat banal mould-blown salt-cellars began to appear, often of rectangular shape. *See* Cut glass.

Salvers: the silver salver, which began to be made in England shortly after 1650, was defined in a dictionary of 1661 as 'a new fashioned peece of wrought plate, broad and flat, with a foot underneath, and is used in giving Beer, or other liquid thing to save the Carpit or Cloathes from drops'. Silver, as usual, was first in the field, but circular glass salvers of similar form probably appeared soon after, the short foot, shaped in both versions like a wide trumpet, being grasped by the person serving the drinks. In the 1680s, references occurred to 'Piramids', and unless the meaning of the term changed in the early 18th century, which is unlikely, it seems evident that the fashion for serving desserts of various kinds from tiers of salvers, which diminished in size from the lowest upward, thus forming a pyramid, was already established in the reign of Charles II.

In an early 18th-century pyramid, the widest and lowest salver often retained the short trumpet foot of the original type, presumably to confer greater stability on the whole structure, but by 1740, the stem was usually as tall as on other varieties.

Salvers of the late 17th and early 18th centuries with the various kinds of knops found on contemporary drinking glasses, are very seldom encountered, but increased production from about 1720 has left a greater number of survivors, mostly with 'Silesian' stems (q.v.) rising from domed and folded feet. The actual flat dish had a narrow border which projected downward as well as upward from about 1740.

Although the Silesian stem generally ceased to be a feature of drinking glasses in about 1730, it persisted on salvers throughout the 18th century despite the introduction of other forms, though the foot beneath it was not always domed or even circular. A pyramid, which comprised three or more salvers for the display of jelly glasses and so

Salver, c. 1740

forth, was commonly surmounted by a stemmed sweetmeat utensil, often known as the 'top glass', which contained dry confections such as orange chips, which were probably the most popular. Sometimes, however, this glass was replaced by a very small salver which was intended to hold a large preserved fruit.

Like other glassware of good quality, some salvers were embellished with cut decoration of a restrained and simple kind from about 1740, and 'large salvers' were mentioned among the items of 'curious cut glass' listed on the trade card of Thomas Betts (q.v.) shortly before the middle of the 18th century. But few cut salvers have survived, whereas plain specimens are comparatively numerous. Among the latter, of the second half of the 18th century, may be mentioned an unusually large variety which turned on a heavy ormolu pivot.

From just before 1800, some salvers were equipped with flute-cut stems mounted on square feet, and these continued into the Regency period. By this time, pyramids had declined in popularity, possibly owing to numerous accidents arising from their precarious construction. Large individual salver-like objects were fashionable in the Victorian era as cake-stands: a role which virtually deprived them of their status as salvers.

Stemmed salvers are sometimes absurdly misdescribed by the Italian word *tazza*, which means a cup.

Sang, Jakob: *See* Newcastle upon Tyne.

Scent bottles: small bottles of varying shape to hold perfumes were a commonplace of ancient Egyptian, Syrian and Roman glass production, but although the identity of early British examples was probably frequently disguised under the term 'vials', they were of little account until the second half of the 18th century.

They were in numerous forms, but a common feature was the small silver or gilt-metal cap which covered the ground stopper in the short cylindrical neck. Some were in cut glass, occasionally colourless, but more often blue, purple, green, or opaque white, the enamelled decoration being manifestly inspired by Sèvres porcelain. After 1770, some blue-glass scent bottles were charmingly decorated with plants and birds in gold, the tonal and chromatic contrasts being extremely effective. Although these are all commonly called 'Bristol', it seems likely, from the similarity between the ornament and the work of certain contemporary metropolitan jewellers, that many of them were made in London.

After 1800, the general enthusiasm for heavily cut glass affected scent bottles as much as anything else, and some of them were so deeply incised that they looked like pieces of coarse jewellery. In addition to cut decoration, many bore finely-modelled busts in crystallo-ceramie (q.v.), which greatly enhanced their appearance.

Toilet-water bottles (q.v.) followed a similar evolution, but may be distinguished by their larger size and the absence of a metal cap on the stopper.

Schurterre: a family of French glass-makers, possibly of partly Germanic extraction, who began to work at Chiddingfold in Surrey in 1343, and continued to produce Wealden glass up to about the middle of the 16th century. Apart from window-glass, it was probably all of a pale green colour.

Sealed glasses: these belong to the early years of British lead crystal. In May 1677, George Ravenscroft (q.v.), official maker to the Glass Sellers' Company (q.v.) of London, began to apply a seal to his glasses in the form of a raven's head impressed in relief on a small pad of glass (*see* Roemer). After his death in 1681, other manufacturers used seals, which can seldom be identified, until about 1685, even on glasses without the lead ingredient; but the manufacture of lead crystal all over

Britain increased to such an extent that the practice eventually ceased to be considered desirable as a sign of quality.

Seed: minute bubbles often occurring in old glass, owing to the fact that furnace temperature could not be raised high enough to drive out all air and gases from the molten mass.

Serving-bottles: bottles made of ordinary dark-toned glass, often bearing seals with their owners' initials, used for serving wine at table before and after the introduction of flint-glass decanters in the last quarter of the 17th century.

Serving-rummers: unusually large rummers (q.v.) of the late 18th and early 19th centuries used for serving toddy (q.v.). They were a later equivalent of constables (q.v.).

Servitor: a subordinate member of a glass-making team or 'chair', who performed ancillary functions such as attaching the pontil (q.v.).

Shaft-and-globe: a modern descriptive term applied to a glass object such as a decanter (q.v.), when it has a globular body and a neck in the form of a narrow cylinder.

Sham drams: deceptive glasses (q.v.) for spirits which occurred in the 18th and 19th centuries. The notion that they were all used by tavern-keepers when offered a drink by a customer must be discounted, since, during the Regency (q.v.) period, they were often made in sets, in the form of small rummers of excellent quality. These had bucket-shaped bowls, sometimes flute-cut, and knopped stems, and were equal in all respects to the best domestic glassware. Those who preferred them to ordinary spirit glasses, with minute bowls hollow right down to their bases, probably did so because their overall size was much greater and they therefore looked more important. *See* also Toastmasters' glasses.

Shanks: an 18th-century name for the stems of glasses.

Ships' decanters: Naval and Mercantile officers liked to use elegant glassware as much as landsmen, but the use of ordinary decanters (q.v.) was impracticable in the unstable conditions prevailing on board ship. Until the last quarter of the 18th century, they were accordingly obliged to make use of wide serving-bottles (q.v.), but special decanters were then devised made of crystalline flint glass.

These had broad bases, sometimes over 30 cm in diameter, and bodies with a triangular profile tapering to the base of the neck, which might be cut, plain or have three or four applied neck-rings. After 1780, they were often called *Rodneys*, as a compliment to the celebrated Admiral who won the Battle of Cape St Vincent in that year, capturing seven enemy ships out of eleven. Cut decoration, when present at all, tended to be slight until almost the end of the Georgian period (1830), and often consisted of little more than fluting (q.v.) on the upper part of the body or neck. Occasionally, a Rodney might be engraved with a sailor's head.

Apart from the triangular shape, some were in the form of broad-mouthed bells, or were nearly triangular but with short vertical sides at the base.

There are large numbers of modern reproductions, and although they are unconvincing to initiates, inexperienced purchasers should always request a written guarantee of authenticity with an approximate date, when acquiring an ostensible ship's decanter. Reputable dealers will be pleased to comply with such a request.

Ships' glasses: these appeared at about the same time as firing glasses (q.v.), from which earlier examples are sometimes indistinguishable, but were provided with wide, thick feet, not so that they could be banged on the table, but so that they would be less likely to slide off it in foul weather. As it was unnecessary for them to withstand frequent concussion, they were able to be made in greater variety than firing glasses and with thinner stems, though most of them were short, to keep the centre of gravity low. They had plain, air-twist, opaque-twist, or cut stems, and a great variety of bowl shapes. *See* Overstrung foot.

Shoulder knop: a small knop, usually spherical, at the top of a stem.

Shouldered decanters: these first appeared in about 1745 as an alternative to the existing mallet-shaped decanters, from which they differed in having shoulders which, instead of being almost horizontal, sloped downward at an angle of about 45°. The bodies varied slightly in shape. In a few instances, the sides were vertical, but in general, they sloped either outward or inward to the base. Although a pouring-lip occurred on a few rare examples, this feature was uncommon on any kind of decanter until after 1770.

Shouldered decanters might be either plain or cut, and were the first type to be engraved, or more rarely enamelled, with imitation bottle tickets denoting the contents. These were known at the time as 'label decanters'. *See* Cut glass and Decanters.

Silesian stems: an incorrect but almost universally-applied term denoting stems of drinking glasses and other objects, formed in a mould and widening upward to angular shoulders. The type probably reached England from the Hanoverian glasshouse at Lauenstein, and first appeared on the accession of King George I in 1714. The earliest, which was also the simplest, was of square section, and sometimes had loyal inscriptions on the shoulders, in moulded lettering, such as 'God save King George', which were doubtless prompted by his coronation in 1715. Some of these had straight-funnel bowls (q.v.) with thick bases, like many glasses of the late 17th century, but other popular forms were the bell and the thistle (q.q.v.), the latter being particularly successful with Silesian stems of all kinds.

The square-section or four-sided type was quickly followed by versions with six and eight sides, then stems which were reeded and, finally, reeded and twisted. Small moulded pyramids sometimes occurred on the shoulders, and a wide, incised collar might encircle the base just above the foot.

Silesian stems generally ceased to be associated with drinking glasses in about 1730, but persisted on candlesticks (q.v.) into the second half of the 18th century, and on salvers (q.v.) throughout the Georgian period. Although the design was unknown in British glass-making before about 1714, it had occurred on Venetian glasses, and on silver wine cups made at Augsburg and Nürnberg, in the 17th century. In origin, it was probably an angular rendering of the inverted baluster (q.v.). *See* Stems.

Skinkers: *See* Spout pots.

Slickers: another name for linen-smoothers (q.v.).

Smelling bottles: small pocket phials with ground stoppers, containing aromatic vinegar, or, in the 19th century, ammonium carbonate mixed with scent. 18th-century smelling bottles were probably intended not only to serve in a restorative capacity, but also to mask the many ill-favoured stenches which abounded; while those made from the second quarter of the 19th century were chiefly to relieve symptoms of faintness, either real or simulated. It is not known precisely when they first began to be made, but their use was widespread by 1750, and it is on record that a consignment of smelling bottles in coloured, cut glass was sent from London to Birmingham in 1752. They were made of opaque white glass from about 1760, and in glass of Nailsea (q.v.) type from the last decade of the 18th century. After 1800, they were sometimes profusely cut.

Splits: a cutting design consisting of incisions made with a mitre-wheel, that is, a wheel with a triangular-section edge. Stars and other patterns could be built up by arranging splits in various ways. After the introduction of the neo-classical style, known also as the Adam style, they frequently occurred in horizontal rows: a device of Roman origin. *See* Cut glass.

Spout pot, c. 1685

Spout pots: these were made in silver, pewter, and glass in the 17th century. Spout pots of glass consisted of two-handled cups with baluster-shaped or straight-sided bodies, with a swan-neck spout which rose from near the base of the vessel and curved outward at about the level of the rim. They were known otherwise as skinkers (q.v.). They have become associated, without satisfactory evidence, exclusively with the service of posset or caudle. *See* Posset pots.

Standing bowl: a large bowl supported on a stem and foot.

Standing dish: a dish supported on a stem and foot, or on a stem which broadens out to form a foot. Rare examples in both soda glass and lead crystal have survived from the 17th century, one, probably by Ravenscroft (q.v.), being like a large soup-plate with applied gadroons (q.v.) underneath, and with a trumpet-shaped stem like that of a contemporary silver salver. The mouth of the trumpet forms the foot. Standing dishes occurred hardly at all after the early 18th century, possibly because salvers and bowls (q.q.v.) were considered adequate alternatives; but they were restored to some sort of favour in the Victorian period, when they were mostly of excellent quality.

Stems: the stems of drinking glasses, considered in this section, displayed features which occurred on other stemmed objects such as candlesticks, sweetmeat glasses, etc., but which did not necessarily occur at the same time. They fall chronologically into the following categories, which are discussed further under their respective headings.

BALUSTER STEMS: the inverted baluster and true baluster occurred with Venetian-inspired glasses made in Britain prior to the introduction of lead crystal in 1675; but thereafter, up to the end of the 17th century, stem forms included only the Inverted Baluster, the Drop Knop, the Angular Knop, the Ball Knop, the Acorn Knop and the Double Knop, apart from a few short-lived types such as the Quatrefoil Knop. (*See* Flutes.)

After 1700, appeared the True Baluster, the Annulated Knop, the Mushroom Knop, the Cylinder Knop and the Ovoid Knop.

All the foregoing were of heavy construction, and although differing in form are generally classified as baluster stems.

Inverted baluster stem, c. 1685

Drop knop, c. 1685

Angular knop, c. 1690

Ball knop, c. 1690

Acorn knop, c. 1690

Double knop, c. 1700

True baluster, c. 1705

Annulated knop, c. 1710

Mushroom knop, c. 1710

Cylinder knop, c. 1710

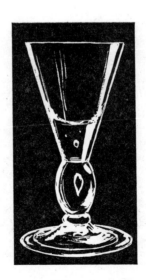

Ovoid knop, c. 1710

LIGHT BALUSTERS: these are often called 'balustroids' (q.v.), and were introduced in the first decade of the 18th century as an alternative to the expensive heavier types. This is known from the comments of a German visitor who, in 1710, went to a London tavern where a lusty fellow named Cherbourn amused the customers by singing and shouting

Light baluster, early 18th century

Light baluster, early 18th century

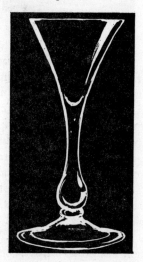

Light baluster, early 18th century

at glasses until they broke. They included not only examples with a 'thick knob', but also 'various fine stemmed glasses'. The late W. A. Thorpe believed that the latter included thin, plain stems (wire stems), but although any opinion from that quarter must be treated with respect, the weight of probability seems against its being correct. *See* Newcastle upon Tyne.

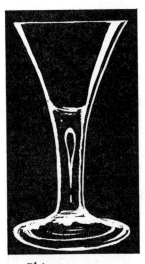

Plain stem, c. 1715

Plain stem, c. 1720

PLAIN STEMS: 'Wire stems', drawn from trumpet-shaped bowls, had occurred in the 17th century in soda glass, though one can never be certain whether survivors are English or Dutch; but what appear to be the earliest of the species in lead crystal were of very robust construction and displayed the same feeling as the heavy balusters, despite the absence of knops. They probably arrived on the scene in about 1710, and increased in popularity so rapidly, that by 1730 their manufacture was on a truly formidable scale. Trumpet and waisted bell-shaped bowls (q.q.v.) were normal in the early stages, when the second had thick bases, but other varieties were used as well, as they came into fashion. The thick, cylindrical stems, set on folded feet, often contained a tear-shaped air-bubble. With the passage of time, they became slimmer. The group included firing glasses and toasting glasses (q.q.v.), the term 'wire stems' being applicable to the latter.

Silesian stem, four-sided, c. 1715

SILESIAN OR MOULDED STEMS: these were introduced in about 1714, and comprised four-sided, six-sided and eight-sided pedestals formed in a mould. They were followed by reeded, then reeded and twisted, versions.

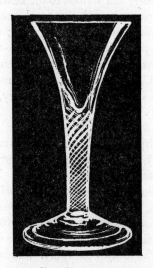

Air-twist, c. 1735

Knopped air-twist, c. 1740

183

Double-series air-twist, c. 1750   *Composite: air-twist and plain, c. 1755*

AIR-TWISTS: these were an English invention of about 1730. Air-twist stems contained spiralling threads of air, and the earliest accompanying bowls were trumpet-shaped. Knopped versions appeared in about 1740, made at first in one piece with the bowl, which was often bell-shaped and waisted, then made separately and welded to the bowl and the foot. Slightly later, double-series twists were devised, and consisted of one series of twists spiralling round another in the centre; these stems were usually, though not always, made separately. Triple-series twists were also known, but their incidence was very small. Mercury, or mercurial, twists, which appeared in about 1750, consisted mostly of no more than two large, brilliant spirals. In the 18th century, air-twist stems were known as 'wormed'.

OPAQUE-TWISTS: probably inspired by the air-twists, opaque-twists, which were introduced in about 1745, consisted of spirals of tin-oxide enamel, and existed in single-series and double-series form, the latter being by far the more numerous. For many years, the enamel was entirely white, but after about 1765, the twists might be in various colours, a mixture of white and coloured, or occasionally coloured and air-twist. Opaque-twist stems were made separately, and had the bowl of the glass welded to one end and the foot to the other. Some were knopped.

184

Opaque-twist stem, double-series, c. 1760

CUT STEMS: there is some evidence which suggests that the stems of drinking glasses might have been decorated by cutting in the first quarter of the 18th century, but even if this is so, there appear to be no survivors from before about 1745. The first design consisted of shallow,

Cut stem, c. 1750

Cut stem, knopped, c. 1760

concave facets of diamond shape, followed soon after by similar facets in the form of hexagons. Both were extremely popular. The stems which they embellished were drawn from the base of the bowls and were mostly cylindrical, though knops sometimes occurred in the second half of the 18th century and were positioned either a short distance below the bowl or in the centre of the stem. Cut facets shaped like scales appeared in about 1760, but scale-cut stems were never anything but rare. Diamond and hexagonal facets persisted at least until 1800, but cut fluting (q.v.) was introduced in about 1770 and was found on both cylindrical and knopped stems. These vertical flutes were sometimes horizontally sliced or notched across the dividing ridges. Fluted stems continued to exert an appeal far into the 19th century.

Incised twist, c. 1755

INCISED TWISTS: these consisted of spiral incisions on the outside of a stem, and were current for only about fifteen years from the mid-18th century. Accompanying bowls were often dimpled or otherwise ornamented.

Stipple engraving: *See* Engraving, stipple.

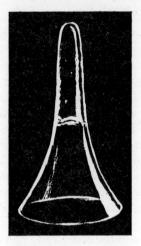

Glass stirrup cup, c. 1720

Stirrup cups: these were glasses without feet for serving liquor to horsemen in the saddle, usually at a hunt, and provide a rare instance of silversmiths following the glass-makers. Certain elaborate glass vessels designed in this manner were made in the late 17th century, but their purpose is uncertain and they may have been purely decorative.

In the first quarter of the 18th century, however, they began to be made for use at a 'lawn-meet', and consisted generally of trumpet, funnel, or waisted-bell bowls from which the cylindrical stem was drawn in one piece and was simply rounded-off at the bottom. Shortly before the middle of the century, the bowl might be in the form of a bucket or waisted bucket, and all these types continued up to about 1770. Thereafter, they were identical with coaching glasses (q.v.), and had a knop at the base of the stem.

Refreshment before a hunt was considered desirable, especially in the Winter, for, in the 18th century, a hunt usually met before first light. A contemporary round by Somerville begins: 'A southerly wind and a cloudy sky proclaims it a hunting morning, Before the sun rises away we'll fly. . . .'

Stoppers: the only stoppers of any comparative stylistic importance were those associated with decanters (q.v.), from which many have become separated in the course of time. It is known that Ravenscroft (q.v.) furnished his decanters with stoppers in the reign of Charles II, but very few have survived. One decanter of this period, of shaft-and-globe shape and with a handle, has a stopper in the form of a hollow cone, fitting loosely into the neck, surmounted by a finial comprising several diminishing horizontal rings, the lower two of which are impressed with gadroons (q.v.). The other contemporary type of decanter, which was like a jug, had a wide mouth and consequently, a larger stopper. The hollow cone went even further down inside the neck, and the broad finial was somewhat like a dome, covered with bold, vertical gadroons. Both of these kinds of stopper had a projecting process at the top which provided an anchorage for the pack-thread by which the stopper was attached to the decanter while it was awaiting sale.

The mallet-shaped decanter of the early 18th century may have had a stopper with a ball-finial which sometimes contained small air-bubbles, but it is widely suspected that many of these stoppers may have been later additions, so that some uncertainty surrounds the matter. Many such decanters may not have had stoppers at all.

Shouldered decanters, introduced in about 1745, were provided initially with a stopper with either a spire-shaped finial or a finial in the form of a narrow, flat-topped cylinder. These were superseded, shortly before 1760, by finials in the form of a flat, vertical disc or a kite, both of which persisted into the 19th century. From about 1780, the disc might have a circular depression on each side and bevelled edges, and this type is sometimes called a 'bull's-eye' stopper. Others, with grooves radiating from the centre of each face, are often called 'target-stoppers'. The mushroom finial appeared in about 1780 and continued far into the 19th century. It had the advantage of keeping dust off the mouth of the decanter. A modified version, known as 'turned out', competed with it from just before 1820, and differed in having a profile like that of a wide-mouthed trumpet instead of being flat underneath the 'cap' of the mushroom.

In the late 1820s, the spire-shaped stopper, plain or cut, returned to some degree of favour, but was appreciably larger than its 18th-century predecessor. It continued into the Victorian era, fighting a losing battle with heavy ball-finials, which appeared in about 1830, and a more bulbous variant of the mushroom with a finial like a compressed sphere. Nearly all these kinds of stopper, arising from about 1760 onwards, were used also in connection with toilet-water bottles.

Stourbridge: dispersed immigrant glass-makers from Lorraine, who had been brought into England by Jean Carré (q.v.), founded the glass industry in the Stourbridge district of Worcestershire in the first quarter of the 17th century; it was soon absorbed by Sir Robert Mansell (q.v.). At this period, Stourbridge was concerned primarily with the production of window-glass, though common green vessels and bottles were made as well, the manufacture of the latter being facilitated by the quality of a local clay which was supremely suitable for melting-pots.

By 1695, there were five glasshouses in the area making flint glass, and it was probably shortly before this that lead crystal was introduced there. Many difficulties were encountered initially, and the task of the nascent industry was made no easier by the imposition of a heavy tax which was not withdrawn until 1699 (*See* Glass Excise Act); but by the mid-18th century, Stourbridge had begun to produce some of the finest metal (q.v.) in the kingdom.

In 1751, Dr Richard Pococke wrote: 'Stourbridge, famous for its glass manufactures, especially for its coloured glass, with which they make painted windows. . . .' Excellent cut glass began to augment the fame mentioned by Pococke from about 1759, and from the last decade of the century, Stourbridge was among several glass-making centres which manufactured variegated objects in the style associated with Nailsea (q.v.). High standards were maintained throughout the 19th century and have endured to the present day.

Straight-funnel bowl: the bowl of a drinking glass with straight sides, widening from the base to the rim. *See* Bowls of glasses.

Straw shanks: when the plain, cylindrical stems of 18th-century glasses were drawn from the base of the bowls without a joint, they were described as straw shanks; they are known also as 'drawn stems'. *See* Stuck shanks.

Strawberry diamonds: a cutting design of the early 19th century. Each consisted of a flat-topped diamond with bevelled edges, the plateau being cut or cross-hatched with a field of very small diamonds, often sixteen in number. *See* Cut glass.

Striae or striations: minute, multiple internal streaks in the substance of glass, indicating a lack of homogeneity, often due to insufficiently high furnace-temperature. Early glass frequently displayed the defect, but it was still very common in the early 19th century, for example, in the thick bases of the bowls of certain rummers (q.v.).

Stuck shanks: an 18th-century term for stems of glasses which were made separately and welded to the bowl and foot.

Sulphides: *See* Crystallo-ceramie.

Sunderland Bridge rummer, c. 1800

Sunderland Bridge rummers: Sunderland Bridge over the river Wear was opened in 1796, and locally-made rummers, especially with bucket-shaped bowls, were often engraved with a picture of the bridge with a ship sailing beneath it. This design continued to be engraved, often in a perfunctory fashion, well into the 19th century, the execution being superior when the event commemorated was fresh in the minds of all concerned.

Sussex: *See* Camden, William.

Swags: a neo-classical design, sometimes engraved on glass in the late 18th century, consisting of looping festoons. It occurred more frequently in architecture, silver and furniture. The name derives from an old English verb meaning to droop.

Sweetmeat glass, c. 1710

Sweetmeat glasses: many different kinds of glass vessels were employed as utensils for what may be broadly classified as sweetmeats or desserts, from the end of the 17th century. In this section, we are concerned with the most important species to attract the attention of amateurs of old glass, namely, sweetmeat glasses mounted on stems and feet and with bowls that were almost invariably wider than those of drinking glasses. It is usually to this variety that the term is applied.

Very few have survived from the last quarter of the 17th century and it is probable that production was on a limited scale. Some had baluster stems like those of contemporary drinking glasses, while others had broad, trumpet-shaped stems of the kind found on the earliest salvers and standing dishes. There are many more survivors from the early 18th century onward, due, no doubt, to the fact that many more were made to satisfy a constantly increasing demand. An especially popular type had a wide bowl which narrowed suddenly inward to a conical base. This was set on a stem with an annulated knop (q.v.) as the dominant feature, usually with a slim inverted baluster beneath it playing a subsidiary role. The foot was commonly of domed formation and with a folded edge.

Sweetmeat glass, Silesian stem, c. 1720

When the so-called Silesian stem (q.v.) was introduced in about 1714, it was quickly adopted as a support for sweetmeat glasses. The four-sided variety is rarely encountered in this connection, but all the other versions were called into service, and although they had fallen out of fashion with drinking glasses in about 1730, they persisted into the second half of the 18th century with the utensils under discussion. Possibly, this was because they endured also with salvers (q.v.), with which sweetmeat glasses were often associated. They were frequently accompanied by ribbed, double-ogee bowls with horizontally-flanged rims which might be given undulating edges, and it is this type of vessel which certain writers have often classified quite dogmatically as a champagne glass. Their only grounds for doing so appear to be first, that it was luxurious-looking and monumental, and accordingly a fitting utensil for an expensive wine, and, secondly, that a common later type of champagne glass, introduced in about 1830, had a wide, shallow bowl. The proposition is thus wholly unsupported by cogent evidence, and is discounted by the fact that the glasses in question often had a capacity at least twice that of a normal wine glass.

It was necessary, for obvious reasons, that drinking glasses should have level rims, but since sweetmeat glasses from which dry confections were taken with the fingers were not subject to the same limitations, some of them, from the first quarter of the 18th century, might be decoratively shaped or have vertical glass loops applied round the edge. The latter were functional as well as ornamental, for they increased the capacity of the bowl without making it look too bulky.

Cut bowls, sometimes mounted on Silesian stems, have survived from the 1730s, and although air-twist and opaque-twist stems occurred at the same time as cut stems on drinking glasses, the cut sweetmeat glasses of the second half of the 18th century are widely considered as the aristocrats of the whole group. They existed in considerable variety and were sometimes equipped with covers like some of their plainer predecessors.

Bowls were of numerous forms and might be cut all over and have edges which were scalloped, serrated, or shaped in other ways. Stems, which were cut with diamond or hexagonal facets, might be cylindrical or knopped, while the feet were often not only cut on the upper surface, but also shaped round the edge. Such plethoric luxuriance would have been unsuitable for a drinking glass, partly concealed by the hand of the user whether he held it by the stem or the foot; but a large sweetmeat glass was meant to remain loftily in its own station and have its contents lifted from the top, and in these circumstances, some degree of dignified opulence was not inappropriate.

The incidence of stemmed sweetmeat glasses declined rapidly after 1800.

T

Tale glass: impure glass from the top of the melting-pot, used to make cheap vessels, especially for use in taverns.

Tankards: a tankard is a drinking vessel with a single handle and a lid, usually hinged. Glass tankards have always been rare in Britain, one of the earliest, which dates from the second quarter of the 16th century, comprising a globular body with a wide, cylindrical neck imported from Venice, and containing white tin-oxide enamel arranged in broad, vertical stripes, divided by lines of clear glass. The lid, hinge, and foot-ring, which is crimped over a projecting flange on the base of the glass vessel, are of English silver bearing the London hall marks for 1548. As stated, however, the glass portion is exotic, only the mounts being of native origin, and it appears that importations of this kind did not succeed in stimulating a domestic production of similar vessels which could be accurately described as tankards.

Other silver-mounted tankards of the 16th century were made of stoneware, horn, or marble, but tankards wholly of silver or pewter were far more numerous then and later.

These facts are mentioned because there is a widespread tendency to use the word 'tankard' in a loose, incorrect manner for what should properly be called a can or mug (q.v.), namely, a single-handled pot without a lid. An examination by the author of numerous bills and inventories has not revealed a single reference to a British glass tankard, though mugs were mentioned frequently in the 18th century. An advertisement by Jerom(e) Johnson (q.v.) in 1751 included the item 'large glasses for cool Tankards'. This does not say, however, that the tankards themselves were made of glass, and the 'large glasses' were presumably cisterns in which tankards could be left standing in cold water to cool their contents. *See* Cans or mugs.

Tapering decanters: known also as taper or tapered decanters, these were introduced in the late 1760s, and had tall, narrow bodies widening from neck to base over shoulders which were scarcely perceptible. *See* Decanters.

Tapersticks: miniature candlesticks (q.v.).

Target stoppers: a modern name applied to vertical disc stoppers, chiefly of decanters and toilet-water bottles, impressed with thin radial gadroons. These stoppers were prevalent in the late 18th and early 19th centuries. *See* Stoppers.

Tazza: the Italian word for a cup. It is mentioned here because the term is sometimes misapplied, by persons who are unaware of its meaning, to flat, circular salvers or shallow standing dishes, on stems and feet. The use of ignorant jargon of this sort is to be deplored. *See* Salvers.

Tea caddies or canisters: the term 'caddy', which began to be used in about 1770 to denote what had been known previously as a canister, derives from a Malay word *kati*, which was a weight of just under 1¼ lb. Tea was exported from the Orient in wooden boxes holding this amount, and the term was eventually transferred from the quantity to the container.

Glass caddies, which began to become fairly popular from the mid-18th century, were mostly in the form of vases, bottles with screw-caps, or square boxes, any of which might have silver mounts. The vase types were often cut with the same diamond, hexagonal, and scale facets found on other glassware, but those in the form of boxes usually had flat sides, each of which, from the late 1760s, were frequently cut with an elaborate but shallow star motif which covered most of the surface. The bottle versions, which tended to be flattened rather than of circular section, might be in enamelled blue or opaque glass, and occasionally, in the style associated with Nailsea (q.v.).

Tears: elongated bubbles of air in the stems or thick bases of certain bowls of glasses, found from the late 17th century.

Terraced feet: these first appeared on candlesticks of the end of the 17th century, but were very uncommon until they began to form part of dram (spirit) glasses from the 1720s. They are so named because the top of such a foot was formed with concentric steps or terraces, angular at first, and rounded later. They also occurred to some extent on other objects.

Thistle bowls: these were of two main kinds. (a) A bowl of a drinking glass of the early 18th century of straight-funnel shape in the upper part, but swelling out suddenly into a solid ball of glass at the base. *See* Bowls of glasses. (b) A drinking-glass bowl of the early 19th century, occurring first in Scottish glasshouses, with concave sides widening into a hollow ball-base. *See* Thistle drams.

Thistle dram, c. 1810

Thistle drams: these spirit glasses first appeared in about 1810, the hollow thistle-shaped bowls being mounted on short stems. In the centre of the stem was a small knop of ball, annular, or bladed type (q.q.v.).

Toasting glass, c. 1735

Toasting glasses: these appeared on the scene in the 1730s, and were of similar proportions to certain soda glasses with 'wire' stems which enjoyed some popularity in Holland in the late 17th century. The bowls were trumpet-shaped, and the tall, thin stems, which were only about 7 mm in diameter, were drawn in one piece with the bowl, the plain foot being welded to the base. They owed their fragile construction to their purpose. After an important toast, the stem was snapped between the user's fingers and the glass was thrown away. A few unused examples have survived, but these glasses are now very uncommon.

Toastmaster's glass, c. 1750

Toastmasters' glasses: these were introduced in about 1740 for the use of professional toastmasters. Most of them were in the form of contemporary cordial glasses, and had tall, straight stems which might be of plain, air-twist, or opaque-twist type, and very rarely cut. The bowls, however, were deceptive, and had a small funnel-shaped hollow in the centre which held only a minute quantity of liquor. The design was doubtless conditioned by unfortunate experiences, for it was the duty of a contemporary toastmaster not only to announce the toasts but also to drink them himself. If his glass had been of normal capacity, he would have become incapable, as the evening wore on, of discharging his duty in a dignified manner. Toastmasters' glasses were made singly and from metal (q.v.) of the finest quality. *See* Sham drams.

Toddy: this term derives from a Hindi word for a palm-tree. The drink was known in England at the beginning of the 17th century, and a travel-book of 1605 referred to 'Palmita wine, which they call Taddy'. This Oriental beverage must have been imported into Britain to some extent, for the fermented juice of various kinds of palm-tree was subject to excise. In the second half of the 18th century, however, the word began to be used in a different and more familiar sense, for Grose's *Dictionary of the Vulgar Tongue* (1788), defined it as follows: 'Toddy, originally the juice of the cocoa (*cocoa-nut*) tree, and afterwards rum, water, sugar and nutmeg'. The original meaning was forgotten by the early 19th century, for it was stated in the *Sporting Magazine* in 1808: 'Punch is certainly wholesomer than toddy, which is grog with the addition of sugar'. Georgian definitions were liable, of course, to be incomplete, and it is evident that toddy existed in several versions, broadly analogous to very strong punch (q.v.), but mostly without the limes or lemons which made the latter 'wholesomer'. Gin or whisky might provide the spirituous element instead of rum. Toddy, in the later sense, was often served with glass toddy-lifters (q.v.).

Toddy-lifter, c. 1800

Toddy-lifters: glass pipettes, about 16 cm long, with bulbous bases and with or without neck-rings, used for serving toddy as an alternative to miniature silver ladles with whalebone handles. It is not known precisely when toddy-lifters first came into use, but it was almost certainly after the word 'toddy' (q.v.) changed its meaning, probably in about 1770. At all events, no surviving examples appear to be earlier than this and the vast majority are later. The user held the toddy-lifter so that the bulbous portion was immersed in the liquor in a serving-rummer. When it became filled through the hole in the base, the thumb was pressed over the hole in the top, and the toddy-lifter was then taken out of the liquor. The contents could not escape while the user's thumb remained in position creating a vacuum, but when it was raised, with the instrument held above a glass, the toddy ran out. By this means, all members of the company received an identical quantity.

Some writers have stated that toddy-lifters were used from the early 18th century for serving wine, but it appears likely to the present author that they have allowed themselves to be beguiled by the earlier significance of the word 'toddy'. In any event, it was the practice in Britain, from the late 17th century, to serve wine from decanters or serving-bottles – into which it would be quite impossible to insert a toddy-lifter – and not from open vessels, the use of the latter postulating a liquid which was compounded for the occasion.

Toddy-sticks: sometimes known by the modern term 'sugar-crushers', these were small metal or glass spatulas for stirring toddy, usually shaped somewhat like paddles. They are mostly impossible to date with any certainty, and the majority of survivors are probably Victorian.

Toilet-water bottles: somewhat similar to scent bottles, but larger and with glass stoppers like those of decanters rather than with metal caps, toilet-water bottles were popular from the second half of the 18th century. Many were cut, some had crystallo-ceramie (q.v.) plaques in the early 19th century. They were chiefly of circular, square, or oval section, and are occasionally indistinguishable from small decanters.

True baluster stems: stems of various objects, particularly drinking glasses, shaped like architectural balusters.They had occurred in soda glass in the 17th century, but first appeared in lead crystal after 1700. *See* Stems.

True baluster

Tumblers: originally, small silver beakers, with heavy rounded bases, which rocked or tumbled from side to side when knocked, instead of falling over. These first appeared in about 1625 and continued to be made to some extent in the 18th century; but even while they were familiar objects in the late 17th century, the name began to be used in its general modern sense, and was misapplied to a particularly stable form of flat-based beaker which nothing could have induced to 'tumble' back and forth.

Shapes varied, but early glass examples tended to have a high kick (q.v.) in the base and to display wrythen surface-decoration. A concave-sided form began to become popular in about 1740, and some are found with Jacobite engraving.

Survivors are more numerous from the late 18th and early 19th centuries, better examples being engraved, or cut with fluting (q.v.) and other patterns such as small relief diamonds. Plain specimens are often difficult to assign to their period of origin, but, in general, the better the quality and colour of the glass, the later the date. Some tumblers were made of 'Nailsea' (q.v.) glass. *See* Beakers.

V

Venice: when Aquileia on the North-Eastern mainland of Italy was sacked by Attila in A.D. 452, the city of Venice began to be raised on piles in the lagoon by the refugees.

It is not known precisely when her later famous glass industry was founded, but it was undoubtedly well established by the end of the 12th century. A hundred years later, it had expanded to such an extent that all glass-makers were obliged by the authorities to transfer their activities to the island of Murano in the lagoon, to avoid the danger of fire in the city itself. By the early 14th century, a significant export trade was developing, and for nearly three hundred and fifty years thereafter, Venetian glass dominated the markets of Europe. Fearful penalties were prescribed for any Muranese glass-workers who offered to carry their skills elsewhere; but such restrictions can never be effective indefinitely, and emigrant craftsmen assisted in the establishment of Venetian-style glass-making in many parts of Europe including the wealthy duchy of Burgundy. The fact is highly relevant to the early history of the British glass industry. *See* Carré, Jean.

Verzelini, Giacomo or Jacopo (1522–1606): despite the severe sanctions prescribed by the Venetian authorities, many craftsmen quitted Murano in the 16th century and secured greater rewards by carrying their glass-making skills to the duchy of Burgundy and elsewhere. Among these emigrant Venetians was Verzelini, who went first to Antwerp, then to England in 1571.

He is a figure of the utmost significance in the history of British glass. He worked initially under the aegis of Jean Carré (q.v.) until the latter's death in 1572, but in 1575, he was granted a patent by Queen Elizabeth I for twenty-one years, 'for the makyne of drynkynge glasses such as be accustomablie made in the towne of Murano', with the undertaking that he should teach the art to the Queen's 'naturall Subjectes'. The licence safeguarded his position further by banning the importation of foreign glass of a similar kind. Verzelini thus had a virtual monopoly in the production of glasses in the Venetian style, though we have it on the authority of Harrison, Camden and others that much green, non-crystalline glass like German *Waldglas* (forest glass) was turned out for a less affluent sector of the native market.

Several of Verzelini's more important glasses are still in existence, and doubtless owe their survival to the fact that they were not ordinary domestic drinking vessels made in sets, but individual goblets decorated by diamond-point engraving and of special significance to their owners and their descendants. The bowl of the earliest, which is dated 1577, is engraved with a hunting scene in the upper zone, with other ornament below, the stem, unfortunately, being a wooden replacement two or three hundred years old. Another, dated 1578, bearing decoration of a similar kind, is complete, the stem being embellished with a hollow, compressed ball knop with vertical gadroons (q.v.). The engraved decoration was probably the work of Anthony de Lysle, who also engraved pewter. Some influence of contemporary English silver-smiths' work is discernible in various aspects of the overall design of several of the glasses.

Goblet by Verzelini, 1578

Verzelini retired in 1592 a very wealthy and respected man. He died in London but was buried in the parish church at Downe in Kent, where he was commemorated by a brass which is still to be seen.

He must receive credit for initiating the manufacture in Britain of glass of high quality, and establishing a norm and a tradition which enabled Sir Robert Mansell in the 17th century to lay the foundations of a national industry.

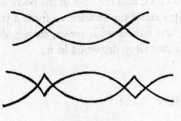

Vesica pattern

Vesica pattern: a decorative design consisting of horizontal pointed ovals, linked directly to each other or with small diamond-shapes intervening, much used by glass-cutters and engravers in Cork from 1783, especially on decanters. The Vesica, or *vesica piscis*, is of ancient origin, and is found in vertical form in early Oriental and Christian iconography as a glory round the heads of sacred personages. It also occurred in the same form as that used by the glass-makers on the pierced stretchers of 'Chinese' chairs in the Chippendale style in the 1750s.

Volunteer glasses: drinking glasses, chiefly rummers (q.v.), engraved with reference to various bodies of British and Irish volunteers which were formed at the outbreak of the war with revolutionary France in 1793. Most surviving examples date from the early 19th century.

W

Waisted bowls: bowls, particularly those of stemmed drinking glasses, which have a zone between the base and the rim which is narrower than either. *See* Bowls of glasses.

Wasp-catchers: known also as fly-catchers, these glass vessels, which were current from about 1790 until the second half of the 19th century, had something of the appearance of wide decanters. They were supported on three small feet, and the base of the body was open, with the sides of the opening extending upward to form a trough about 5 cm deep. This trough was baited with sweet, strong ale which attracted vexatious insects so that they drowned in it.

Water jugs: *See* Jugs.

Waterford: a small glasshouse was in operation near Waterford in the first half of the 18th century, but it was short-lived and its few productions are unidentifiable. Although the Glass Excise Act of 1745 (q.v.) and subsequent legislation which reinforced it, imposed no taxes on Irish glass, only British glass was allowed to be imported into Ireland, and the export of any glass whatsoever was banned. In 1780, however, the ban was lifted, and this changed the situation completely. Realizing the competitive advantages with the new circumstances created, two Irish gentlemen, William and George Penrose, established a glasshouse in the city in 1783 with a capital of £10,000, receiving a grant from the Irish Parliament to cover the initial expense of building and equipment. The Penrose brothers were businessmen, but evidently knew nothing about glass-making, nor were they able to find Irish craftsmen to staff the new factory. They therefore induced John Hill, of the Golbourn-hill Glasshouse near Stourbridge in Worcestershire, to go to Waterford and pioneer their venture, and Hill took with him 'the best set of Workmen he could get in the County of Worcester'.

It will be seen from these facts that Waterford glass of the late 18th century should be regarded as British glass made in Ireland, though this does not, of course, imply any criticism of Irish craftsmanship. Hill returned to England in 1786 and was succeeded as factory-manager by Jonathan Gatchell, who implemented existing policy with such success that Waterford glass found important oversea markets including the United States. In 1799, the Penrose brothers sold the business to Gatchell and his two partners, Borcroft and Ramsey, and the new owners transferred operations to another glasshouse which they built in Old Tan Yard. By 1811, Gatchell was in sole possession, and died in 1823 leaving a flourishing venture which remained in his family until the glasshouse closed down in 1851.

There is documentary evidence which leaves no doubt that great trouble was taken to ensure that the glass produced by the Waterford factory was as crystalline and free from tint as possible, despite a legend started by Hartshorne in his *Old English Glasses* (1897) that it displayed a 'pale blue tinge'. This myth has been disposed of by M. S. Dudley Westropp, upon whose researches most of our knowledge of Irish glass is based. He had a vast experience of the subject and stated that he had never seen a single marked authentic Waterford specimen which showed the defect in question. It is difficult to imagine what moved Hartshorne to make his unfounded pronouncement, which has caused an amount of trouble which he could never have envisaged.

Waterford decanter with arch and rectangle design, c. 1800

The blue tinge, which was due to the inadvertent use of impure lead oxide, occurred with some frequency in glass produced in Dublin and Cork, and since certain early 19th-century decanters from the latter source were almost identical with those made in Waterford, Hartshorne may have been deceived by the similarity into making a rash, inaccurate statement in a book which was otherwise careful and scholarly.

One result of his lapse was that large numbers of reproduction Waterford decanters, deliberately coloured blue with cobalt oxide, were made in Europe in the 19th and early 20th centuries, and these are still cherished with careful pride in various countries including the United States. They have even been produced, on occasion, as tangible proof that the myth was fact! The forgeries in question are always marked underneath with the words PENROSE WATERFORD. This inscription often, though not always, occurred on the bases of genuine decanters and jugs from the late 18th century, even after the Penrose brothers had ceased to have any connection with the factory, and was imparted by reversed lettering in intaglio arranged in a circle on the internal bases of the moulds into which such lower-grade objects were blown. Free-blown Waterford specimens, which were better finished and altogether superior, were never marked at all, and are consequently difficult to distinguish from glass made elsewhere. This applies particularly to the many varieties of drinking glasses, which were more or less identical all over the British Isles.

With cut glass, however, some assistance is rendered by certain designs which were especially popular in Waterford. First among these in importance is the Arch and Rectangle design, consisting of round-headed arches filled with fine diamonds, springing from rectangles embellished in the same manner. It appears that this design did not occur in England or Scotland and is therefore a strong evidential factor. Another frequent pattern was a circuit of curved pendants below a horizontal line, forming segmental compartments which were also cut with small diamonds. It was of British origin, and sometimes appeared in the form of engraving just below the rims of certain wine glasses before and after 1770, but was very seldom found on decanters and jugs of the last two decades of the 18th century and the early 19th century except in Ireland.

Many other designs, such as small linked diamonds in a horizontal band, were used as well, but as they occurred on glass objects from many other sources, they are not conclusive evidence of a Waterford origin.

Some of the best productions of Waterford were large standing bowls, one type, with a circular receptable having a turned-over edge, being usually described as a fruit bowl, another of boat-shape being considered as a salad bowl. Both were sometimes spoilt by the proportions of the stems and feet, but they were often very handsome objects indeed and superior to anything made in Scotland or England. (*See* Bowls.)

Chandeliers used to be regarded as one of the most outstanding manufactures of the Waterford glasshouse, but this view is now discounted, as it is known that many of the cut lustres from which the chandeliers were built up were made in Birmingham and merely assembled in Ireland, though they were undoubtedly assembled in a very imposing manner.

The Waterford industry was eventually ruined by taxation. The extension of the Glass Excise Act to Ireland in 1825 slowly undermined this very worthy Anglo-Irish venture by destroying its competitive position, for the heavy, untaxed crystal to which it had previously been so devoted, now involved it in as much expense as any other glasshouse in Britain. It is deducible from this that the earlier success of Waterford was based, not on quality alone, but on quality combined with price.

A magnificent display of Waterford glass was seen at the Great Exhibition in 1851, but this proved, in the event, a mere heroic gesture, for the glasshouse ceased operations later in the same year.

It is unfortunate that the importance of the factory should have come to be unnecessarily exaggerated. There is far more so-called Waterford glass in existence than the glasshouse could possibly have manufactured, for its production represented only a small proportion of the total output of the British Isles.

Waterloo Company: *See* Cork glass.

Welt: another name for the fold occurring on the feet of some stemmed glasses.

Wheel-engraving: *See* Engraving.

Williamite glasses: these were counter-Jacobite glasses engraved, after the 1745 rising, with designs pertaining to King William III (1689–1702) including portraits. In Ulster, their significance was politico-religious, and they remained popular there, especially among Freemasons and Orangemen, throughout the 18th century.

Wine-glass cooler, c. 1800

Wine-glass coolers: individual wine-glass coolers appeared in the second half of the 18th century in glass. They contained cold water in which glasses were inverted to cool the bowls. Some were in transparent blue or opaque coloured glass, but the majority, which date from the late 18th and early 19th centuries, were in colourless crystal and bore cut decoration. They were mostly of the same size and appearance as finger bowls, from which they were distinguished by having one or two pouring-lips; but in the late Regency, a type was found mounted on a short stem and foot and looking somewhat like a rather tall rummer, but still with a pouring-lip.

Winged knop: *See* Quatrefoil knop.

Witch balls: these were about 15 cm in diameter and were hung up to ward off the evil eye. In the early 18th century, they seem to have been called 'watch bottles', presumably because there was a small neck at the top by which the ball was suspended and which gave it a slightly bottle-like appearance. Later in the century they were known as 'watch balls', the short neck having disappeared and been replaced by a hole for a plug. They were frequently coloured in the second half of the 18th century, blue being probably the most popular, but towards 1800 they might be in glass of Nailsea (q.v.) type. Witch balls were not silvered inside until the mid-19th century.

Wolff, David: *See* Newcastle upon Tyne.

Wormed shanks: an 18th century name for air-twist stems (q.v.).

Y

Yard of ale: it is not certain when these long ale glasses were first made in Britain, but they undoubtedly existed in the reign of James I (1603–25) under the name of 'ell glasses'. Doubtless the term was used loosely, for an ell is nine inches longer than a yard. In February 1685, John Evelyn recorded in his diary that after the accession of James II had been proclaimed in Kent by the High Sheriff, the new King's health was 'drunk in a flint glass of a yard long', and the poet Lovelace, in the middle of the century, had already mentioned 'Elles of beare'.

These glasses had feet, and were functional, if somewhat *outré*, drinking vessels; but in the 18th century they assumed the form of the trick glasses of which many examples – mostly later reproductions – are still to be seen in English taverns. The lower part of the stem terminated in a hollow bulb, and as an unpractised user raised the glass higher to drain it, air rushed into the bulb and squirted the remainder of the contents in his face. Many of these glasses are quite modern.

BIBLIOGRAPHY

ANGUS-BUTTERWORTH, L. M. *British Table and Ornamental Glass*, 1956.
ASH, DOUGLAS. *How to Identify English Drinking Glasses and Decanters 1680–1830*, 1962.
BATE, P. *English Tableglass*, 1905.
BEDFORD, JOHN. *Bristol and Other Coloured Glass*, 1964.
BLES, J. *Rare English Glasses of the 17th and 18th Centuries*, 1920.
BUCKLEY, FRANCIS. *A History of Old English Glass*, 1925.
CHARLESTON, R. J. *English Opaque White Glass – 18th century*, 1962.
DAVIS, DEREK. *English and Irish Antique Glass*, 1965.
DILLON, E. *History of Glass*, 1907.
ELVILLE, E. M. *English Tableglass*, 1951.
—*English and Irish Cut Glass*, 1953.
—*A Collector's Dictionary of Glass*, 1961.
FLEMING, A. *Scottish and Jacobite Glass*, 1938.
FRANCIS, G. R. *Old English Drinking Glasses*, 1926.
GUTTERY, D. R. *From Broad-Glass to Cut Crystal*, 1956.
HARTSHORNE, A. *Old English Glasses*, 1897.
HAYNES, E. B. *Glass through the Ages*, 1948.
HONEY, W. B. *English Glass*, 1946.
HUGHES, G. BERNARD. *English Glass for the Collector*, 1958.
—*Table Glass in England, Scotland and Ireland*, 1956.
LEWIS, J. S. *Old Glass and How to Collect It*, 1916.
PELLATT, A. *Curiosities of Glassmaking*, 1849.
POWELL, H. J. *Glassmaking in England*, 1923.
RUGGLES-BRISE, S. *Sealed Bottles*, 1949.
SAVAGE, GEORGE. *Glass*, 1965.
THORPE, W. A. *A History of English and Irish Glass*, 1929.
—*English Glass*, 1935.
WAKEFIELD, HUGH. *Nineteenth Century British Glass*, 1961.
WESTROPP, M. S. D. *Irish Glass*, 1920.
WILKINSON, O. N. *Old Glass*, 1968.
WILMER, D. *Early English Glass*, 1910.
WINBOLT, S. E. *Wealden Glass*, 1933.